A Positive Approach to the International Economic Order

Part I: Trade & Structural Adjustment

by Alasdair MacBean

Professor of Economics
University of Lancaster

BRITISH-NORTH AMERICAN COMMITTEE

Sponsored by
British-North American Research Association (UK)
National Planning Association (USA)
C.D. Howe Research Institute (Canada)

ISBN 0-902594-33-8
Library of Congress Catalogue Card Number 78-70406

Published by the British-North American Committee
Produced in the United Kingdom by
Birn, Shaw & Co. Ltd, London EC1 1AL

October 1978

Contents

A POSITIVE APPROACH TO THE INTERNATIONAL
ECONOMIC ORDER
PART I: TRADE & STRUCTURAL ADJUSTMENT
by Alasdair MacBean

Statement of the
British-North American Committee
to Accompany the Report

Over recent years the BNAC has become more and more concerned over the increasing politicisation of discussions between the developed and developing countries on what has come to be known as the New International Ecomonic Order. It has seemed to the Committee, as a group of people concerned primarily with economic issues, that the polemics that have come to dominate international discussions tended to conceal what the Committee believes to be the underlying community of interest in furthering the economic development of one group of countries and in meeting the needs of the other group for materials, some of which are essential to their economies[1].

We therefore asked Alasdair MacBean, Professor of Economics at the University of Lancaster, to take a fresh and objective look at the realities of the problems underlying the debate and to put forward proposals to meet two criteria which we thought were necessary for any lasting solution. These were that they should:

1. Be practical and constructive, and designed to promote co-operation rather than merely avoid conflict; and
2. Be consistent with the basic principles of the market economy and the most efficient use of scarce resources for the benefit of the world as a whole.

We now present the first part of a study by Professor MacBean which we believe to be an important contribution to clarifying the difficult issues which underly the debate. In particular, this report examines the likely effects on developing countries of international commodity agreements and compensatory financing schemes, and explores the problems surrounding the opening of the developed countries' (DCs) markets to imports of manufactured goods from developing countries (LDCs). The author's proposals cover:

· Reform of agricultural protection in developed countries to admit more produce from developing countries and reduce dumping of agricultural products from DCs in world markets[2].

---

1 *I would also point out that markets in the developed countries are obviously essential to the LDCs if many of the materials they produce are to be of value to them.* — **Ian MacGregor**

2 *I believe that the consequences of applying the policies advocated in this paper to domestic agriculture need further study. A good economic case can no doubt be made for leaving the production of some foodstuffs, such as sugar, to the less developed countries, but the social, political and strategic disadvantages of withdrawing protection or support from domestic agriculture on a significant scale may well outweigh the economic advantages. The worst feature of the Common Agricultural Policy must certainly be eliminated, but it seems unlikely any Government will ever agree to policies which could lead to a serious decline in their own food supply.*—**A.C.I. Samuel**

- Increasing provision by developed countries of financial and technical assistance to less developed countries in the production, preservation, processing and transportation of food and raw masterials.
- Reduction of tariffs and non-tariff barriers to LDC exports of processed materials and commodities.
- Greater efforts within the GATT by a number of LDCs to secure access for their manufacturers on a MFN basis instead of seeking greater but limited access through the generalised system of preferences.
- Complete re-examination of adjustment assistance programmes in developed countries for both people and firms, to include safeguard procedures, and administration by semi-autonomous agencies.
- The setting up of an international grain reserve to alleviate the effects of famines especially in least developed countries

The Committee appreciates the magnitude of the change in attitude that will be required of politicians, businessmen, and trade union leaders in both developed and developing countries if these and similar proposals are to be implemented. Although the economic benefits to the world economy are apparent, solving the political problems inherent in some of the proposals will require considerable statemanship. We believe that our three countries could if they so willed give the necessary leadership.

The issues dealt with in this first paper do not, of course, cover all the matters of concern to developing countries. The investment policies and general activities of multinational corporations, the amount and direction of aid by the richer nations to those less developed, the use and availability of technical knowledge and the working of the world finaincial system are but four other themes for polemical debate in international organisations. We hope to publish a second paper next year which will analyse these areas of policy in the same constructive spirit which we believe this first paper shows.

While not necessarily endorsing in detail all the author's views and suggestions, we believe his work is a valuable contribution to an important subject.

FOOTNOTES TO THE STATEMENT AS A WHOLE

In signing this statement, with much of which I agree, I must nevertheless say that I do not think the case against international commodity agreements has been made at all conclusively, especially as regards agricultural products. I do recognize that every commodity poses special problems and difficult areas which must be addressed. In the case of some commodities an agreement may not be negotiable, and other approaches will have to be substituted. Nevertheless, progress must be made toward a better world economic order with improved stability and equity of returns to producers and producing countries. In this I believe commodity aggreements have an important role to play. In grains the objective of holding adequate internatonal reserves for food security must be combined with provisions to protect producers' returns and to contribute to price stability. One without the other is neither equitable nor feasible. — **Charles Munro**

I do not think the summary of Professor MacBean's proposals as given in the Committee Statement adequately reflects the healthy skepticism which he expresses in his study in regard to the desirability and efficacy of certain programmes which are popular in much of the developing world. — **Nathaniel Samuels**

While agreeing with Professor MacBean's logic, I have no doubt that the developing countries are firmly committed to the idea of a common fund and commodity agreements. If the richer countries do not go along with these plans, there is no doubt that the relationship between north and south would be severely strained. — **Lord Seebohm**

Members of the Committee Signing the Statement

Chairmen

SIR RICHARD DOBSON
President, B.A.T. Industries, Ltd.

*IAN MacGREGOR
General Partner,
Lazard and Frères and Co.
Honorary Chairman, Amax Inc.

Vice Chairmen

SIR ALASTAIR DOWN
Chairman,
Burmah Oil Company

GEORGE P. SHULTZ
President, Bechtel Corporation

Chairman, Executive Committee

WILLIAM I. M. TURNER, JR.
President and Chief Executive Officer,
Consolidated-Bathurst Limited

Members

J. A. ARMSTRONG
Chairman and Chief Executive Officer,
Imperial Oil Limited

See footnote to the Statement

G. R. HEFFERNAN
President,
Co-Steel International Limited

ROBERT HENDERSON
Chairman, Kleinwort Benson Ltd.

ROBERT P. HENDERSON
President and Chief Executive Officer,
Itek Corporation

JACK HENDLEY
General Manager (International),
Midland Bank Limited

HENDRIK S. HOUTHAKKER
Professor of Economics,
Harvard University

TOM JACKSON
General Secretary,
Union of Post Office Workers

DEAN DONALD JACOBS
Graduate School of Management,
Evanston

JOHN V. JAMES
President and Chief Executive Officer,
Dresser Industries

GEORGE S. JOHNSTON
President, Scudder, Stevens & Clark

JOSEPH D. KEENAN
President, Union Label and Service
Trades Department, AFL-CIO

TOM KILLEFER
President, United States Trust
Company of New York

CURTIS M. KLAERNER
Executive Vice President and Director,
Mobil Oil Corporation

H. U. A. LAMBERT
Vice Chairman, Barclays Bank Limited

WLLIAM A. LIFFERS
Vice Chairman,
American Cyanamid Company

J. P. MANN
Deputy Chairman
United Biscuit (Holdings) Ltd.

WILLIAM J. McDONOUGH
Senior Vice President,
The First National Bank of Chicago

DONALD E. MEADS
Chairman and President
Carver Associates, Inc.

SIR PETER MENZIES
Welwyn, Herts

JOHN MILLER
President,
National Planning Association

DEREK F. MITCHELL
Chairman and Chief Executive Officer,
BP Canada Limited

JOSEPH P. MONGE
Rancho Santa Fe

DONALD R. MONTGOMERY
Secretary-Treasurer,
Canadian Labour Congress

MALCOLM MOOS
St. Paul, Minnesota

*CHARLES MUNRO
President, Canadian Federation of
Agriculture

KENNETH D. NADEN
President, National Council of
Farmer Cooperatives

WILLIAM S. OGDEN
Executive Vice President,
The Chase Manhatten Bank, N.A.

See footnote to the Statement

Abbreviations used in this Paper

ACP	African, Caribbean and Pacific Countries associated with the European Community
CAP	Common Agricultural Policy of the European Community
CFS	Compensatory Financing Scheme
DAC	Development Assistance Committee of OECD
DC	Developed Country
GATT	General Agreement on Tariffs and Trade
GDP	Gross Domestic Product
GSP	Generalised System of Preferences
ICA	International Commodity Agreement
IMF	International Monetary Fund
IPC	Integrated Programme for Commodities
LDCs	Less Developed Countries
MFN	Most Favoured Nation
MTN	Multilateral Trade Negotiations
NIEO	New International Economic Order
OECD	Organisation for Economic Co-operation and Development
OMAs	Orderly Marketing Arrangements
OPEC	Organisation of Petroleum Exporting Countries
QR	Quantity Restrictions
TA	Technical Assistance
TEA	US Trade Expansion Act 1962
UNCTAD	United Nations Conference on Trade & Development
UNDP	United Nations Development Programme
VERs	Voluntary Export Restrictions

Author's Preface

For many years the representatives of developing countries have complained of inequities allegedly inherent in the international economic system. Pent up frustration with the failure of the rich nations to keep their promises in the field of aid or to give way to demands for various reforms in trade formed the background to the sixth Special Session of the General Assembly of the United Nations in 1974. Flushed with the success of the OPEC nations in turning the tables upon the industrial countries in the battle for the economic rents from oil production, the developing countries demanded the creation of a New International Economic Order. But a new era did not dawn. For over four years the debates have continued, but little progress has been made towards meeting the aspirations of the developing countries. Yet the issue, involving as it does the conflict between poor nations with over two thirds of the population of the world, and the relatively rich nations, is certainly important, perhaps crucial, to the continued peace and prosperity of the world community as a whole.

The objectives of this first section of this study are to analyse the implications of various policy proposals which have been put forward at UNCTAD and elsewhere to promote the aims of the developing countries in the field of international trade and to consider some alternative policies. The results of that analysis suggest that the net gains to developing countries from such policies as international commodity agreements or further possible improvements in the generalised system of preferences, are likely to be small. Policies aimed at reducing barriers to trade in both primary and manufactured exports of interest to developing countries promise much more substantial gains to them, but should also benefit the developed countries.

In the long run the majority of nations and of the citizens of both poor and relatively rich countries should gain from reductions in trade discrimination and the promotion of free movement of goods, services, capital and technology, but the forces for protectionism are strong in all countries. The present levels of unemployment and imbalance in trade among the rich nations are inhibiting further movement towards free trade. It is very much in the interest of the developing countries to throw such influence as they have in favour of freer trade more generally. Any tendencies towards protectionism in the industrially developed nations would be seriously damaging to developing countries. The history of free trade areas and customs unions among developing countries does not suggest that such 'go-it-alone' policies contribute much to the solution of their trade problems though they may help in the longer run.

I am grateful to the British-North American Committee for suporting my work on this topic and for the comments, suggestions and encouragement which I have received from the members. I am particularly grateful to Mr F. Taylor Ostrander and Dr Dermot McAleese for some detailed comments on a late draft of the paper. Simon Webley and Melanie Jones have supplied unstinting administrative assistance and moral support in preparing for the various BNAC meetings. The Washington office of the BNAC was also very helpful in arranging meetings with US Government and World Bank Officials with whom I had useful discussions in December 1977. My thanks go to all of these people for their help. None of them, nor the BNAC collectively, of course, bears any responsibility for the contents of this paper.

1st September 1978   A. I. MacBEAN
                                                   University of Lancaster

The Author

Alasdair I. MacBean is Professor of Economics at the University of Lancaster. In 1973-4 he was Visiting Professor at the University of Michegan, Ann Arbor. He has been an economic advisor in the Harvard Development Advisory Service, and in the British Ministry of Overseas Develoment; he has also been specialist advisor to the House of Lords Select Committee on Commodity Prices. He has been a consultant to various UN agencies, OECD and USAID.

Professor MacBean is the author of a number of works in the field of economic development including *Export Instability and Economic Development* and *Meeting the Challenge of the Third World*.

A Positive Approach to the International Economic Order

Part I Trade and Structural Adjustment

by Alasdair MacBean

I.   INTRODUCTION

A.   Objectives and Proposals

The desire for a New International Economic Order (NIEO) springs from dissatisfaction with the Old. The clamour for radical change at the Sixth Special Assembly of the United Nations in 1974 was triggered by the oil producing nations in dramatically raising the price of their oil exports and changing the balance of economic power, but the fundamental causes ran much deeper. The Group of 77, in their proposals for a New International Economic Order are simply following a tradition in post World War II thinking on development which stresses adverse impacts from existing international economic relations upon their economic prospects, specifically:

● They believe that the income which they receive from exports of primary products is both lower and less stable than it should be. They are suspicious of the activities of transnational companies, believing that too little of the returns from their investments accrue to the host economies, that the companies fail to transfer appropriate technology to the developing countries, that they exert too much political power and generally exploit in various ways their superior expertise and commercial muscle in dealings with less developed countries (LDCs).

● They believe that the prevailing system of international economic relations not only lowers their earnings from the export of agricultural and mineral products, but that it discriminates against their desire to industrialise through processing these new materials for export in more advanced forms.

● They note that the rich countries profess a belief in free international trade but act to protect industries which compete with developing countries' exports, especially in textiles, clothing, leather goods and footwear. The rich nations proclaim the virtues of free markets for LDCs' exports such as cocoa, coffee and tea while busily intervening to support and stabilise the prices and producers' incomes in their own agricultural markets for butter, sugar, cereals, meat, fruit and wine.

● Developing countries have observed that the major decisions on finance and official aid are taken in fora in which they have little direct say. Yet they have special interests in these matters which differ from and sometimes conflict with the interests of the rich nations.

Considering all this, it is not surprising that they are critical and blame the system for many of the failures which they have experienced and the difficulties which they face in attempting to raise the standard of living of their citizens. They view the NIEO as the way to remedy the inequity of the existing system.

The thinking of many leaders in the LDCs has been conditioned by the colonial experience and by the analyses of writers such as Marx, Hobson and Lenin in earlier years and more recently by Prebisch and Singer. Thus they see trade and investment between rich and poor nations in terms of economic imperialism and regard institutions such as the World Bank, the IMF and the GATT as props of that system. This colours the rhetoric and even influences the proposals. But it should be recognised that most of the proposals for a NIEO are reformist, not revolutionary. Many go back in origin to Bretton Woods, to the still-born International Trade Organisation and its concern for international commodity agreements. As we move away from the heady atmosphere of the Resolutions of the Sixth Special Assembly of the UN, pragmatism and more sophisticated analyses of detailed proposals become more evident[1]. In a cooler atmosphere it should be recognised that progress towards the general objectives of development and equity is more likely to be achieved by recognition of common ground, possibilities of trade-off between gains and losses, by negotiation rather than confrontation. The OECD nations could help to promote such an atmosphere if they would come forth with genuine proposals of their own to assist the LDCs rather than merely fighting a rear-guard action against the Group of 77s' proposals.

General objectives such as improved economic growth, increased employment and a more equal internal distribution of income in the developing countries are broadly acceptable to leaders in rich and

---

1.   "Co-operation between industrial nations and the rapidly advancing countries of the Third World is entering a new phase — a phase of constructive realism. The period of 1974-76 will be viewed in retrospect as one of transition to a 'New Realism'", Maurice Williams, Chairman of DAC in "Development Co-operation: Efforts and Policies of the Development Assistance Committee, 1976 Review". (OECD, Paris, November 1976).

poor nations alike. It is over the means to achieve these objectives that real differences of opinion arise. The intention of this paper is to select proposals which are in the long run interest of both rich and poor countries. The gains to the LDCs are likely to be much greater than any likely to emerge from the proposals which they have stressed at UNCTAD and elsewhere. Indeed, this paper will contend that the trade policies most emphasised by the Group of 77 are unlikely to work, and even if they did work, their net effects on the welfare of LDCs could prove adverse and would almost certainly bring them little benefit. Alternative policies designed to promote the freer movement of goods, capital and technology promise greater benefits both to LDCs and to the world at large.

Some of the recent proposals for a NIEO are acceptable and should be welcomed. There is no objection in principle to increased flows of official aid beyond the derisory amounts to which, in real terms, aid has fallen in recent years[2]. Perhaps more important, a reduction in the tying of aid to source suppliers would increase the value of aid to recipients and reduce the importance of a major non-tariff barrier in international trade. Other proposals worthy of support are a more equitable distribution of voting power in institutions such as the International Monetary Fund (IMF) and the World Bank, recognising the growth in importance of many LDCs as well as the distinctive requirements and special interests of LDCs in international monetary reform and flows of international finance. Similarly certain improvements in compensatory financing for export fluctuations and reductions in tariffs and all other barriers to LDCs' exports are policies which should be endorsed.

The major points of controversy lie in the fields of trade, foreign private investment and transfers of technology. In these areas the approach of the Group of 77 is one of market management, restriction and intervention. The proposals for trade are set out and examined in the following sections of this paper, and alternative measures for attaining the same basic objectives are put forward.

---

2. Although official development assistance (ODA) from DAC member countries has risen continuously in nominal terms the rise in the prices of aid goods, as a result of general inflation, has meant a fall in the value of aid in real terms e.g. "The real volume of net ODA flow from the United States decreased sharply from around $4,000 million in 1963 and 1964 (at 1970 prices) to around $3,000 million in 1969-72. (Commonwealth Technical Group 'Towards a New International Economic Order,' July 1975, p.41). Also as a percentage of the total GNP of the developed market economies ODA has fallen from 0.51 per cent in 1963 to 0.36 per cent in 1975. (DAC, 1976 Review).

B.   The Current Position on Proposals for a New International Economic Order

Following the initial Declaration on the establishment of a NIEO and the adoption of a Programme of Action at the Sixth Special Session of the UN in April 1974 the debate has continued in various fora. The Seventh Special Session of the General Assembly of the UN in September 1975 saw a shift from confrontation towards conciliation and co-operation between developing and developed countries, but the meeting of the Fourth United Nations Conference on Trade and Development (UNCTAD) in Nairobi in 1976 revealed the divisions once more. As soon as the LDCs attempted to extract definite commitments from the developed countries to an Integrated Programme for Commodities (IPC) including measures to stabilise prices at raised levels, a Common Fund of about $6 billion to finance stocks, diversification and other objectives, indexation of primary commodity prices, improved compensatory financing arrangements and promotion of processing in developing countries, the major developed nations showed their hostility to these ideas.

The United States, the Federal Republic of Germany, and United Kingdom and Japan could not agree that there was any need for radical changes in the existing international order. Only Norway was prepared to pledge money ($25 million) to the Common Fund. Others were willing to support it if the rest would. Canada was not against the principle of a Common Fund, but was not convinced of its usefulness. None of the OPEC nations was prepared to pledge sums to the Fund though they supported it in principle. Despite the look of enthusiasm shown by the developed nations, the proposals emerged in Resolution 93(iv) Integrated Programme for Commodities adopted by consensus. In addition to setting out the multitude of objectives the Resolution laid down a timetable for negotiations to set up a Common Fund, and for meetings to prepare and negotiate international commodity arrangements.

Since UNCTAD IV the developed countries have reduced their opposition to the IPC. At the Conference on International Economic Co-operation in Paris in June 1977 and in subsequent international meetings the idea of some sort of Common Fund has been accepted by them. Disagreement remains over whether it should be confined to the simple role of a source or pool of finance to be drawn upon by individual international commodity agreements for financing buffer stocks or have a 'second window' to finance other objectives, such as construction of commodity storage facilities in developing countries, investment projects in diversification, processing, transportation, and marketing of commodities.

The United States seems to have shifted its policies to be somewhat more favourable to international commodity market interventions. In 1976 the US finally agreed to join the International Tin Agreement, has continued its membership of the International Coffee Agreement, has indicated willingness to participate in the new Sugar Agreement, and is pushing for a more effective Wheat Agreement. Spokesmen for the US Administration have expressed optimism about agreements in natural rubber and tungsten. The UK has at last agreed to make financial contributions to the Tin Agreement and has shifted its position on the Common Fund. Canada seems to have remained non-commital.

Reasons for the more favourable attitudes to the IPC from developed nations are mainly political. The IPC is the main concrete proposal for a NIEO and the Common Fund has been treated by the LDCs as the touchstone of the good faith of the developed countries. Without some softening of attitudes it was felt that discussions on a NIEO would break down completely with the likelihood of disillusionment and bitterness on the part of the LDCs who have zinned exaggerated hopes of improvements in their economic lot on the establishment of a new international economic system. Worries about the possible reactions of oil exporters and some other mineral exporters to a total breakdown served to stimulate a search for compromises. The European Community has another motive in that international measures to support and stabilise prices for sugar and cereals would aid or complement their domestic farm income support policies. There has also been increasing use by politicians of the economic argument that price instability in commodity imports is a cause of inflation in the developed countries.

Despite the diplomatic attempts to gloss over the differences they remain fundamental. The philosophic approach of the Group of 77 remains intensely critical of the operation of market forces on the grounds that the results are inequitable. Most of the developing countries are unlikely to consider efforts to smooth out fluctuations in prices about their market-determined trends or to smooth out LDCs' export incomes a sufficient response. This accounts for their insistence that the Common Fund must be much more than a mere banker to international commodity agreements. Besides which countries like India would be unlikely to benefit from a simple stock-financing role for the Fund, as India's main primary commodity export, tea, faces a problem of a secular decline in its real price, but shows very little price instability.

The position taken in this paper and argued in the following sections is that in practice most aspects of the IPC will prove unworkable and that they would in any case be more inefficient and at least as inequitable as the present international system. Other reforms which stress the importance of maintaining and strengthening market forces in international trade and finance are likely to bring greater gains in economic welfare to both LDCs and the world as a whole.

II. Trade in Primary Commodities

A. Introduction

It is in the field of trade in primary commodities that the NIEO proposals have been most fully worked out. They are recorded at length in numerous UNCTAD documents on the Integrated Programme for Commodities (See Appendix III for UNCTAD, 1976 Resolution on the IPC). The broad objectives are:

(1) to improve the terms of trade of developing countries, and to ensure an adequate rate of growth in the purchasing power of their aggregate earnings from their exports of primary commodities, while minimising short-term fluctuations in these earnings; and (2) to encourage more orderly development of world commodity markets in the interests of both producers and consumers. (UNCTAD, TD/184 para. 11, May 1976).

The main proposals for attaining these objectives are: international buffer stocks, harmonization of national stock policies, measures to manage supplies of commodities including export quotas and production policies, improvement of compensatory financing facilities and improvement of market access for commodity exports of developing countries in both raw and processed forms. The integrating elements in these proposals which differentiate the NIEO from earlier versions of these same ideas are the Common Fund and the simultaneous negotiation and setting up of international commodity agreements (ICAs) for 10 to 18 commodities. (Listed in Appendix II, Table 1).

B. Buffer Stocks and the Common Fund

If it is accepted that there should be international buffer stocks for at least several commodities, and if the Common Fund were simply to act as a banker to the managements of these buffer stocks the idea has some merit. Changes in the prices of commodities are not all in the same direction. Often some rise while others fall. The commodity booms of the Korean War and of 1973 are major exceptions, but even in these the phasing of price swings was not identical for all commodities. Correlations between annual changes in commodity prices are in general quite low and in several cases negative over the last twenty years.[3] This supports the UNCTAD view that there would be some economy in central funding of buffer stocks though the amount saved would probably be relatively small[4].

---

3.   A. I. MacBean and D. T. Nguyen, Mimeo, Lancaster 1977.
4.   Gordon W. Smith, "Commodity Instability: New Order or Old Hat", Paper to conference *Challenges to a Liberal International Economic Order* (Washington, Dec. 1977), Section III, p.25. Jere Behrman, *International Commodity Agreements*, (Washington, Overseas Development Council, 1977) pp. 68-69.

A second argument for a Common Fund is that it pools risks. Some buffer stocks managements may be successful and make profits, others may err in their judgements and make losses. Depending on how the Fund operates, whether it lends to all at the same rates or charges higher rates for buffer stocks with poor records the Fund may either cross subsidise the unsuccessful from the successful or it may act as the agent for the original suppliers of funds and reduce risks. How it operates would affect the rates at which it could obtain marginal funds from the free capital market. There might also be some economies of scale in raising money in larger amounts for a central fund. Finally, once instituted it is expected to act as a catalyst in stimulating the creation of more international commodity agreements by easing their problems of finance[5].

On balance, with the provisos stated at the beginning of this section, the Common Fund might marginally reduce the overall costs of buffer stocks. Most of the disagreements between governments on this issue have centred on what the precise purposes of the Common Fund should be and on how it should run. Many of the LDCs see it as being a force for management of supplies, financing diversifications and coordinating the operations of individual ICAs. Governments in some of the industrial nations are basically opposed to ICAs and therefore are against a Common Fund to finance them. Others do not object to a Fund which would simply act as a banker to the individual buffer stock authorities who would control their own schemes. Yet others feel that the creation of a Common Fund should itself await the setting up of the ICAs, for only then can the sums of money required, be estimated. Some governments in both rich and poor countries might object to contributing to a general fund which could use their subscription to finance some commodity scheme which they had no wish to support.

The UNCTAD estimates the total capital requirements for the Common Fund as $6 million for the ten core commodities plus some others but excluding grains.[6] Almost all independent estimates put

---

5.   Commonwealth Technical Group, *Report on the Common Fund.,* strongly supports the Common Fund.

6.   UNCTAD TD/184, May 1976, p.25.

the figure which would be required much higher. Professor J. Behrman, with rather optimistic assumptions and a reasonable target for stabilisation policies of $\pm$ 15% around long term trend prices, puts it at a minimum of $10.4 billion. Professor Gordon Smith would put it rather higher.[7] The Commonwealth Technical Group notes that firm estimates are not possible, but takes the UNCTAD figure as a reasonable maximum to put on the fund initially, partly because the ICAs will take some time to become active and some will be delayed.[8]

The key issue is whether the ICAs can achieve the objectives stated for them. In particular, if buffer stocks can be successful a Common Fund is a reasonable but probably not very important or practical extra. If buffer stocks are unlikely to work it is largely an irrelevancy.

Buffer stocks cannot permanently raise prices. At best they can smooth out fluctuations in commodity prices. Clearly, this is more relevant to the UNCTAD objective of 'minimizing short-term fluctuations in developing countries' earnings from their exports of primary commodities'. Reduced price fluctuations might either raise or reduce long run export earnings, but such results depend upon the precise market characteristics and causes of the price instability and therefore vary between commodities and even the same commodity over different periods.

The issue raises three basic questions:

● Are short-term fluctuations in developing countries' commodity export earnings a general and significant problem for developing countries?

● Can buffer stocks stabilise primary products' prices?

● If they can, what effects would this have on the stability of LDCs' export earnings?

Are short-term fluctuations generally important?
The answer to the question, despite all the attention which has been given to it, is that for the vast majority of the citizens of the Third World export fluctuations are probably of little significance. Most of the Third World population live in a few large countries where exports are a relatively small proportion of national income and have in any case been relatively stable. Over two thirds of the population of the Third World live in China, India, Pakistan,

---

7. Behrman, *op. cit.* pp. 68-69, Smith, *op. cit.* Section IV, p.24.

8. Commonwealth Technical Group, *op. cit.,* p.40.

Bangladesh, Indonesia and Brazil. For these countries the ratio of exports to national income normally lies between 5 and 10 per cent. Moreover, over the 20 years, 1951-70 their export earnings have been approximately as stable as the average for developed countries.[9] It is implausible to suppose that short-term fluctuation in the prices received for their commodity exports have had significant macro economic effects upon their stability or growth.

A great deal of research has been devoted to the issue of whether fluctuations in export earnings have in general an adverse effect upon economic growth in LDCs.[10] Most studies have used cross-country comparisons to test whether those countries which have experienced the most export instability have tended to have slower growth. A major difficulty is to isolate the effects of export instability from the other variables which influence growth. Probably none of the studies can claim to have truly succeeded in doing this. A recent survey of this literature by Professor Robert Stern concludes "that the case has certainly not been proven that export instability is a serious deterrent to growth in LDCs."[11]

Of course, this does not imply that no developing countries have suffered considerable difficulties from export instability. Countries like Zambia, Chile and Ghana, which are heavily dependent on one or two primary commodity exports, might be expected to face special problems in maintaining a steady flow of imports, stable national incomes and government revenues. For them major slumps in copper or cocoa prices bring economic and political disturbance in their wake. What is rather surprising, however, is that the number of developing countries which combine a higher than average degree of export earnings instability with an export ratio of more than 20 per cent is only about 25. Of these, 10 are mainly oil exporters (more than 50 per cent of their export earnings are from oil), and 3 of the remainder, Hong Kong, Taiwan and Singapore are major exporters of manufactures. Only a relatively few countries involving a very

9.   See House of Lords, *Select Committee on Commodity Prices* (HMSO May 1977). Tables 4.2 and 4.3. Indonesia's exports became much more unstable because of the sharp rise in oil exports after 1972.

10.   A. I. MacBean, *Export Instability and Economic Development* (Allen and Unwin, 1966), P. B. Kenen and C. S. Voivodas, "Export Instability and Economic Growth", *Kyklos* (Fasc. 4, 1972), O. Knudsen and A. Parnes, *Trade Instability and Economic Development* (Lexington Books, D. C. Heath 1975).

11.   R. Stern, "World Market Instability in Primary Commodities", *Banca Nazionale del Lavoro: Quarterly Review* (June 1976) p. 180.

small proportion of the population of the developing countries can be regarded as likely to be very vulnerable to commodity export instability.[12] This would suggest that, even if there were a large number of successful ICAs which moderated instability in commodity prices only a few would derive substantial macro economic benefits. Of course there might be smaller benefits spread more thinly for a much larger number of countries and people.

It has also been suggested that export instability tends to have inflationary effects upon LDCs. One theory suggests that when exports boom governments' revenues rise and they increase their expenditures. When exports subsequently fall the governments, for political reasons are unable to cut back expenditure. They meet the ensuing balance of payments deficit by import controls and the budget deficit by borrowing. This leads to excess demand for domestic output and causes inflation. If true, it would still be questionable whether the culprit is the fluctuating exports or irresponsible government economic policies.

A general conclusion is that most of the people who live in the Third World are relatively unaffected by short-term export instability. There are a number of economies which can be expected to be very much affected and a larger number where export instability may produce certain inconvenience. It must be remembered that short-term instability means movement up as well as down in export revenues. To establish that it is harmful requires that the effects of the downward shifts be more important than the effects of the increases in revenues, or that the uncertainty created by the changes is a significant cost. All economic decisions are taken in the face of uncertainty. If it is known with a fair degree of certainty that export revenues will fluctuate about their trend the fluctuations can be largely discounted. What really matters is the trend. There is no convincing evidence that countries with unstable exports invest less than those with stable exports, nor that primary commodities where prices fluctuate a great deal attract less investment than those where prices are relatively stable. It should also be borne in mind that buffer stocks can only deal with fairly regularly reversed fluctuations about a trend. The costs and the risks involved in holding international buffer stocks to deal with the rare major commodity crises of Korea and 1973-5 puts them outside the realm of practical policies.

---

12.   See House of Lords, *Select Committee on Commodity Prices, op.cit.* pp. XXIX to XXXI and Tables 4.1 to 4.5.

2. Can Buffer Stocks stabilise commodity prices?

The answer is that it is fairly doubtful. The management of a buffer stock has to buy when prices are below trend and sell when they are above it. But the trend itself is unknown. At best they have to work with forecasts which have high uncertainty, at worst, with rules determined by bargaining between producer and consumer governments. If successful they would be doing something which would earn them a fortune as speculators in commodity markets. That professional international civil servants, subject to political pressures and many rules and regulations, should be able to achieve what the private professional speculators often fail to do is somewhat incredible. This is the main technical problem. An error of judgement in setting the floor and ceiling prices for the ICA will either result in the acquisition of excess stocks which eventually have to be dumped back in the market at a loss or if the target prices are set too low the ICA never acquires any stocks and has no effect.

A possible solution in principle is to adopt automatic formulae, of an adaptive forecasting type, to set the limit prices for purchases and sales. Such a formula could include changes in the size of stock itself as one determinant of the buying and selling prices. If the formula adjusts prices quickly to current changes, however, the stock operations will be very limited and it will do relatively little stabilising. If it responds with a considerable lag the previous risk of excess or deficient stocks may arise. Attempts to simulate such policies with past data show that the design of such automatic rules is fraught with difficulty.[13]

Such buffer stock simulation exercises do have rather frightening implications for the capital requirements. One, using the Charles River Associates — Wharton EFA copper model, showed that to have held copper prices within a band of ± 15 per cent of long run equilibrium levels between 1955 and 1974 would have required a maximum copper stock valued at well over $3 billion in 1977 prices.[14] This compares with UNCTAD's Common Fund estimate of $6 million for 18 commodities.

The only example of an ICA which has made use of buffer stocks

---

13.   G. Smith, *op. cit.* Section I pp. 10-11, summarises evidence from previous studies by himself and others.

14.   G. Smith, "An Economic Evaluation of International Buffer Stocks for Copper" October 1975. Department of State/Intelligence and Research, Washington D.C. See also UNCTAD, TD/B/IPC/Copper/AC/1.42 (4th Nov. 1977).

is the International Tin Agreement. It is generally regarded as a qualified success. But the stock of 20,000 tons was never adequate. Although it usually succeeded in defending the floor, this was done by resorting to quotas on exports. The ceiling was frequently breached. A recent article in *The Economic Journal* concludes that it only marginally reduced instability in tin prices and producer incomes. In fact the US strategic stockpile transactions were far more important. To be effective it would have required a maximum stock at least 5 times as large as it possessed. The nerves of the management of an effective tin agreement over the period studied 1956-74 would have had to have been very good to have carried on buying for a sufficiently lengthy period to smooth the lengthy dip in tin price.[15]

ICA's in general have a poor record in price stabilisation. During the Coffee Agreement years 1964-72 the average annual price fluctuation was at least 50 per cent greater than for the non-agreement period 1950-63. Sugar and rubber agreements were destabilising on international prices. Only in wheat and tea could some success be claimed for international agreements. In the case of wheat US and Canadian production and stockpiling decisions and not the agreement were the crucial factor. On the basis of past experience, *a priori* reasoning and simulation experiments it is evident that buffer stocks are hard to negotiate, limited in application to products which are storeable at reasonable cost, and at best only likely to achieve a moderate reduction in price instability, say $\pm$ 15 per cent of trend price, at worst liable to cause more instability through human error.

3. *Effects of Buffer Stocks on export earnings*

However, even if they succeeded in reducing instability in international commodity prices this might do relatively little to moderate fluctuations in individual countries' export revenues. In some cases it could destabilise them and depending on market conditions could either raise or lower average revenues. Some technical analysis of these possibilities is presented in Appendix I but the main issues are quite simple.

A substantial part of the cause of export revenue fluctuations is changes in supply which may be due to droughts, floods, frosts, strikes and political disturbances. Even with a fixed price these

15. G. Smith and George Schink, "The International Tin Agreement: A Reassessment." *The Economic Journal,* December, 1976.

would cause revenue to fluctuate. UNCTAD documents recognise this and recommend compensatory finance as a supplementary stabilisation measure to take care of it. But the situation can be worse than they suggest because for certain commodities the major cause of instability may be shifts in supply at the world level. When Brazil's coffee supply is cut by frost the coffee price rises so that the fall in quantity is wholly or partly offset by the rise in price. A stabilised price in this case would worsen the fall in Brazil's export revenue. A large supplier in these cases would find its export revenues destabilised by a stabilised price. The smaller suppliers faced with a perfectly elastic demand would have less revenue fluctuation with a stabilised price. The welfare effects are quite uncertain: world export revenue is made less stable, the revenues of the large suppliers are made less stable, but the smaller suppliers' revenues are stabilised. A further qualification is that where supply shifts were due to delayed reactions to previous price instability price stabilisation would dampen these and so reduce revenue instability.

If the major cause of fluctuations in price is variations in demand, as is likely for many raw materials, a stabilised price will also stabilise revenue.

The variety of response in earnings to price stabilisation forms an important argument for the case by case approach to ICAs and the need for more research into elasticities and causes of fluctuations before setting up schemes. In practice supply shifts have over the past 25 years probably been at least as important as demand shifts. Until 1972 the economies of the industrial world had maintained very stable rates of expansion of national income. Recessions were very mild. Given the very low income elasticities of demand which are common for most food and raw materials it is implausible that swings in demand should have been very important in commodity markets.[16] Of course we may now be in a much less stable world in which OECD nations' incomes could again be the engine of instability.

The general conclusion from this section is that even if international buffer stocks were remarkably successful in stabilising prices this would certainly not remove all earnings instability and could at least in some cases, increase it. Only a limited number of

---

16.   House of Lords, *op. cit.* Appendix, Tables 3.3 and 3.3 a. There are some qualifications to this as fluctuations in say Russian wheat production appear on the world market as a change in demand for wheat exports.

commodities are really suitable for buffer stocks, as admitted in UNCTAD's own detailed analysis.[17] For example, special attributes and complexity rule out oils and oilseeds; cost, multiplicity of classification of ore and technical problems of location and space for iron ore and bauxite, and perishability for meat and bananas. For others, stocks are regarded as playing only a supplementary role to other measures. A recent study by L. N. Rangarajan gives a harsh judgement on this aspect of the Integrated Programme:

"Of the 18 commodities in the list, the stock mechanism is suitable for four, of which two already have operating mechanisms and one does not need to be stocked in the near future. The mechanism is unsuitable for five. In the case of fibres, the mechanism can perform a limited role; whether it is useful for timber has not yet been analysed. For the rest, the solutions lie elsewhere. It is difficult to avoid the conclusion that the stock mechanism was first chosen as a saleable proposition and the Integrated Programme then fitted round it."[18]

C. Compensatory Finance Schemes (CFS)

It is said that the paramount policy objective of stabilisation policies is the overall export earnings of LDCs so as to improve their ability to maintain domestic income stability and plan for growth. If so, schemes which aim **directly** at smoothing out fluctuations in the total foreign exchange available to them must be superior to ICAs which can only do this indirectly and very partially.

The Compensatory Financing Facility of the IMF was set up in 1963 with this objective. However, access to it was limited by very stringent conditions so that over the twelve years to 1975 the total drawings were only $1.25 billion. But in December 1975 the terms were liberalised. The limit on drawings was raised from 25 to 50 per cent of the member's quota and the maximum permitted amount outstanding raised from 50 to 75 per cent. These and some other minor improvements have made it much more attractive and drawings upon the facility have sharply increased.

The principal upon which such schemes work is that countries can borrow on reasonable terms whenever their exports fall below a target level and should repay the loans when exports exceed that

---

17. UNCTAD, TD/B/C.1/194 "An Integrated Programme for Commodities", October, 1975.

18. L. M. Rangarajan, *Commodity Conflict,* (Croom-Holme, 1978) p. 305.

target. In the IMF scheme the target is set by means of a moving average which includes two previous years, the current year and a forecast for the two subsequent years. The latter were originally constrained to be no more than 10 per cent above the two previous years but this has since changed to permit the projection of earnings for the two following years to assume that earnings grow at the same rate as in the recent past. Simulations of such schemes show that they would have worked in the past to moderate export earnings fluctuations at reasonable costs.[19] Further improvement of Compensatory Financing in the light of experience is almost certainly the best answer to LDCs' problems of export earnings instability.

The European Community's Stabex scheme established under the Lomé Convention is a much more limited version of this approach. It is confined to the African, Caribbean and Pacific (ACP) territories associated with the Community, to a small group of commodities and the sums involved are rather small.[20]

CF Schemes do nothing to stabilise prices. These are left to be determined by supply and demand in world markets. This is at once a defect and an advantage in that attempts by governments or international authorities to control prices have seldom proved on balance beneficial to the community at large. It is a defect in so far as commodity price fluctuations are in themselves a serious economic problem apart from their effect on export proceeds of LDCs. Recently, attention has been focussed on the possibility that they can cause inflation.

Several recent statements by politicians and some academics have put forward the theory that commodity price fluctuations have an important ratchet effect which increases the rate of inflation in developed countries.[21] In the context of the Integrated Programme this seems implausible. Altogether the 10 core commodities form an average 4.4 per cent and the whole 18 commodities only some 9.7 per cent of total imports into the developed countries.[22]

---

19.   T. Morrison and L. Perrez, "Analysis of Compensatory Financing Schemes for Export Earnings Fluctuations in Developing Countries", *Journal of World Development* (1976, Vol. 4, No. 8).

20.   It is severely, perhaps too harshly criticised in David Wall's paper, "The European Community, Lomé Convention: Stabex and the Third World's Aspirations", Trade Policy Research Centre, (London, 1976).

21.   Sir Harold Wilson, speech to Commonwealth Heads of Government, Kingston, May 1975, Lord Kaldor "Inflation and Recession in the World Economy" *The Economic Journal,* December 1976. Jere Behrman, *op. cit.*

Some of the support for these ideas comes from casual association of the commodity boom in 1973 with the worldwide stagflation which has been experienced since, the casual observation that prices in the supermarkets always seem to move up and never down and the acknowledged fact that nominal wages tend to move only upwards. But these observations are consistent with many explanations of inflation. Few could deny that the initiating force in 1972-73 was the simultaneous expansion of the economies of the OECD nations. This met an unlikely combination of events in the shape of failure of the Russian wheat crop, food shortages in India and the Sahelian countries, depletion of US wheat stocks by deals outside the market and by changes in US agricultural policy, destruction of the achovy harvest in Peru, monetary and exchange crises, private and government speculation in commodity stocks. To all this turmoil was added the sudden shock of quadrupled oil prices. If the world had possessed larger stocks of a number of commodities, especially of grain, this would certainly have made some contribution to stability. But normal buffer stocks designed for the fluctuations of 1955-72 would have made little impact upon that situation.

The ratchet hypothesis has been subjected to analysis in a recent article in *The World Economy*.[23] The theory is that increases in commodity prices are passed on to final goods prices on a cost plus basis, but that when commodity prices fall imperfections in market structures prevent a symmetrical reduction on finished products' prices. Another version has the mechanism as nominal wages, and therefore costs and prices, rising when commodity prices rise, but not falling when they fall. Yet, another suggests that the mechanism is that a fall in commodity prices raises profits in manufacturing which triggers wage claims which are conceded, but when commodity price increases squeeze profits, nominal wages do not fall. The authors, Michael Finger and Dean DeRosa subject this to a micro economic test. If finished good prices respond in the way suggested then it should be expected that the processed versions of commodities which would display the fastest rate of increase would be those where the raw material prices are the most unstable. There

---

22.   Commonwealth Technical Group, *op. cit.* Table 2, p.78, average for 1970-75 trade figures.

23.   M. Finger and D. DeRosa, "Commodity-Price Stabilisation and the Ratchet Effect", *The World Economy,* Jan. 1978, pp. 200-1. The test was carried out with both unweighted instability indices and the indices weighted by materials input-output coefficients with the same results of no positive correlation.

should be a positive correlation between the degree of instability of the raw material's price and the rate of increase of the price of their processed forms. But in fact they found no positive correlations for 20 such goods. They also report a number of other studies which have found that cost changes are generally passed on *both* up and down.[24] They conclude that "This is a rare case in which the evidence could be presented by a one-handed economist. Relevant studies 'in the literature' as well as our own test oppose the validity of the ratchet hypothesis. There is no evidence 'on the other hand'".[25]

Their test is not quite as conclusive as they suggest. The mechanism could be of a more macro economic type where a terms of trade improvement due to a fall in commodity prices gives rise to wage increases but when the terms of trade worsen, aggresive trade unions are able to defend their real wages.[26] But that requires synchronised movements in commodity prices of fairly large proportions. Apart from the Korean War and 1973-5 this is not typical of commodity price instability. Given the fact that all 18 of the UNCTAD commodities are only some 10 per cent of Developed Countries' imports and less than 2 per cent of their national incomes, given the Finger and DeRosa evidence, and given the very limited amount of commodity price stabilisation likely to emerge from ICAs it does not seem a very powerful argument in support of the UNCTAD proposals.

The general importance of commodity price instability has probably been exaggerated. Most investment decisions in mining and in plantation agriculture have very long lead times. They are likely to be based on trends and forecasts of future supplies and demands rather than on current prices. Intra year or even year-to-year swings in prices are unlikely to have much influence on sophisticated investors. There seems little if any evidence that short term reversible changes in prices about their trend deter investment. William Fox in his book on the Tin Agreement comments that "Tin

---

24.   Finger and DeRosa, *op. cit.,* pp. 178-9.

25.   Finger and DeRosa, *op. cit.,* p. 201. Goldstein, "Downward Price Inflexibility. Ratchet Effects and the Inflationary Impact of Import Price Changes: Some Empirical Evidence", *IMF Staff Papers* (Nov. 1977) p.608. Comes to similar conclusions with a macro model.

26.   Stuart Harris, Mark Salmon and Ben Smith, "The Analysis of Commodity Markets for Policy Purposes", (Trade Policy Research Centre, Thames Paper, forthcoming) p.51.

does not seem to have attracted the general flow of new capital that might have been expected, and there are no signs that the other non-ferrous metals, without the advantage of a floor price, have found any difficulty in raising capital to maintain or expand production."[27] There may be more of a problem for small farmers, but often the prices they receive bear little relation to international prices because of the intervention of export marketing boards, common in most LDCs.

D.   Some Suggestions for Moderating Price Instability

However, accepting that price instability does cause uncertainty to producers, traders and consumers and so imposes real costs on society, much may be done to moderate price fluctuations and alleviate its effects without the need for elaborate international machinery.

● Governments in LDCs can use marketing boards, stabilisation funds and variable export levies as mechanisms to reduce instability of producers' prices. The availability of compensatory financing to stabilise their foreign exchange receipts makes it much easier for them to follow such policies.

● Improvements can be made in the operation of existing spot and futures markets for commodities.

● Government interventions in both national and international commodity markets which are destabilising can be reduced and reformed.

It ought to be more widely recognised how much commodity price instability is itself the result of government intervention. Huge purchases to create strategic stockpiles for the US government were a major factor in the Korean War boom. Subsequent releases from these stocks, at least in earlier years, were a factor in depressing various commodity prices. In a number of cases commodity exchange prices are merely residual market prices. Sugar is an extreme example of this. Most sugar produced is sold under one or another of domestic and international arrangements which attempt to fix prices. This has the inevitable effect that excess supplies and excess demands have to be absorbed by a relatively narrow free market. The extremely erratic behaviour of international sugar prices is in fact largely the result of the protectionist behaviour of the

27.   W. Fox, Tin: *The Workings of a Commodity Agreement* (Mining Journal Books Ltd. London 1974) Chapter XIX quoted in Rangarajan, *op. cit.* p.233.

rich countries. Reductions in the barriers to trade in sugar, wheat and other temperate zone agricultural products would considerably reduce price instability as well as benefitting consumers in DCs and most producers in LDCs. Centrally planned economies, especially the Soviet Union are equally guilty of causing price instability, particularly in sugar and wheat.[28]

Apart from reducing barriers to trade the markets could be improved through better flows of information, not merely about current supply and demand, but also any factors likely to affect the future: better forecasts of demand, changes in government policies, numbers of trees and their age structure for crops such as coffee and cocoa. The existing commodity exchanges are highly sophisticated markets, which have developed to meet the needs of buyers and sellers to deal with the uncertainties created by commodity instability. It is an area in which there is a great deal of ill-informed suspicion which probably inhibits some producers and governments from making use of future markets to reduce uncertainty. Speculation as an activity is itself misunderstood. A better understanding of its functions in carrying risks could lead to wider use of the facilities with benefit to procedures and consumers alike. Better flows of information can be encouraged by more and better served commodity study groups.[29] Improved information should lead to more stabilising speculation both in holding stocks and in future contracts. There are a number of measures which governments can take to facilitate improvements in the markets. They can have watchdogs to prevent malpractice or to keep self-regulating systems up to scratch. Where necessary they can impose regulations to prevent bankruptcies of dealers which could destabilise markets. They can make use of their controls over credit to prevent excessive amateur speculation which can at times be destabilising. Dissemination of improvements in agricultural technology, wider use of irrigation and plant protection will tend to reduce extreme variations in production of crops.

---

28. D. Gale Johnson, "Limitations of Grain Reserves in the Quest for Stable Prices", *The World Economy,* June 1978, documents the effects on international price instability which arise from attempts to protect and stabilise domestic grain markets.

29. See House of Lords *Select Committee on Commodity Prices, op. cit.* Chapter VIII "Commodity Markets, Speculation and Price Instability" and Recommendation XIX.

E. Price Enhancement

The other major UNCTAD objective in the commodity field is to raise commodity export proceeds. Price stabilisation could contribute to this, but measures to improve the terms of trade, i.e. raise their prices above the levels which would prevail in free markets are clearly in the minds of many in the Group of 77 and are at the base of fears about commodity policies held by nations such as USA, Japan, Britain and Western Germany. Techniques such as export quotas and export taxes have been suggested by UNCTAD as methods of raising commodity prices. Both would operate by restricting the supply of exports. This is a dangerous policy, unworkable for most commodities because of relatively easily available substitutes, and even where feasible unlikely to achieve much in terms of the amounts of revenue transferred from rich to poor countries.

It has to be remembered that developed countries have a much larger share of the export of non-fuel commodities than do LDCs. In 1974 the percentage shares were: developed countries 61.6, LDCs 29.4 and centrally planned economies 9.0. Moreover, the general trend has been for this difference to grow as shown in Table 1.

Table 1

**LDC's Share in World Exports
of Non-fuel Commodities.**

Year	%
1950	50
1955	45
1960	40
1965	35.7
1970	35.4
1974	29.4

A general rise in commodity prices does not necessarily benefit most LDCs. Excluding oil, the developed countries' revenues from exports of commodities rose more in the 1973-74 boom than did LDCs.[30]

---

30. Rangarajan, *op. cit.* p.203.

To effect transfers of resources from rich to poor countries ICAs or Commodity Cartels have to pick commodities which are mainly exported by LDCs as well as meeting the technical market requirements of low price elasticity of demand, few producers and a low elasticity of supply from sources outside the cartel or commodity agreement. Probably none of the metal ores meet the requirements. The possibility of further mineral cartels has been extensively studied since the oil crisis and the consensus is that the conjunction of situations favourable to major cartel action is no longer generally considered to exist beyond the case of petroleum."[31]

Schemes to raise prices have been considered technically possible for coffee and cocoa, and perhaps tea and sugar. They certainly have very low price elasticities of demand and the previous Coffee Agreement may have raised revenue to coffee producers by about $500 million per annum for a few years. But they all face the threat of competition from outside suppliers. The development of corn sugar has probably destroyed sugar's prospects of price enhancement. Such schemes are terribly hard to administer through export quotas. Production is very difficult to control and when surpluses start to emerge governments are apt to cheat. The exporters need the effective co-operation of the importers to discipline their own members. But the importing nations are unlikely to concede much price enhancement and are apt to turn a blind eye on breaches of their own nations' traders. The 'tourist coffee' problems of the Coffee Agreement illustrate the difficulties.

The imposition of a set of uniform taxes on each of a fairly wide range of export commodities would have better prospects of success than the use of export quotas. But it would still be limited by the possibilities of substitution.

A major criticism of either of these routes to price enhancement is that they seek to transfer resources from rich to poor countries in ways which have no relation to either need or ability to make effective use of the resources. The developed countries would be likely to see this as simply an inferior way of providing aid to LDCs and there is a definite risk that they would cut their financial aid by a commensurate amount.

---

31.   British-North American Committee, Report BN19 — "Mineral Development in the Eighties: Prospects and Problems" (1976) pp. 7-9. See extensive list of other studies there.

Both export quotas and taxes function through restricting supply. Many of these commodity exports are labour intensive and regionally concentrated. As such, restricting supply could have serious consequences for domestic unemployment. Unemployment is itself, perhaps, the major problem facing LDCs today and in the immediate future. It exacerbates the risks of starvation and the problems created by excessive migration to the cities.

In sum, neither quotas nor taxes on exports present attractive or practicable means to raise LDCs earnings from exports. In so far as they could work the transfers achieved would be arbitrarily and rather inequitably distributed. Such small gains that are possible would go to better-off nations in Latin-America. They would add to other LDC problems such as unemployment and urban chaos and if they substituted for aid would bring no net resources transfer.

F. An Alternative Approach

An alternative, liberal approach to raising LDCs earnings from commodity production would involve:

● Reform of the industrial nations' systems of agricultural protection so as to improve access for LDCs' commodity exports such as sugar, meat, fruits, vegetable oils and grains and reduce the generation of EEC surpluses which are dumped in world markets and depress prices.

● Financial and technical assistance to LDCs in the production, preservation, processing and transportation of food and raw materials.

● Reduction of tariff and non-tariff barriers to LDCs' exports of elementary processed commodities, in particular, reform of tariff escalation.[32]

Estimates of the potential gains for LDCs from these policies are very large. A recent study from the World Bank estimates that the dismantling of protection for nine major primary commodities would increase the growth rate of earnings from these by 3 per cent per annum. "In fob value terms there would be an increase of $7.1 billion in LDC export earnings from $19.7 to $26.8 billion in 1980 in constant (1974) terms which is equivalent to an increase of about $12

---

32.   Typically the developed countries have zero tariffs on the most basic forms of raw materials and tariffs rise with the degree of processing. This means that the effective protection of the processing in the developed countries is much higher than is implied by the nominal tariffs.

billion in current (1980) terms''. [33] One may take these figures with a pinch of salt, but still recognise that beside them the possible gains from ICA price enhancement is 'peanuts'.

The major problems facing such policies are the protectionist interests in DCs. There are some reasons for thinking that they are weakening and that opposition to reform of the European Community's Common Agricultural Policy (CAP) for example could be overcome. The agricultural labour force in Western Europe has already declined from about 22 per cent of the labour force in 1959 to about 12 per cent today. It tends also to be an ageing group of the population. This both reduces the structural adjustment problem and the voting power of the agricultural lobby. Clearly reforms of the European Community's CAP must be a long-term objective. The political commitment to it is too strong to be overcome speedily. But the system is irrational, damages consumer interests from the viewpoint of efficiency and harms the interests of LDCs, Australasia and North America. Moreover, the CAP was supposed to help poor farmers, but in fact has mainly assisted the large, more prosperous farmers and raised land values to the benefit of landlords. [34]

The industrialised nations themselves would gain greatly from such policies both in terms of reduced real costs of obtaining primary and processed commodities, and in expanded export markets in LDCs as they spent their increased earnings. LDCs would also gain from reduced tariff escalation through their enhanced attractiveness to foreign investment in processing near the source of extraction of minerals. Lower costs of transportation, availability of plentiful supplies of unskilled labour and lower environmental costs make location of metal refining and elementary processing of many raw materials in LDCs an attractive prospect for some transnational companies. This is not always the case. Energy costs, lack of social overhead capital, political risks can offset these factors. Even transport costs do not always prescribe location of processing near source. The question of the gain to both LDCs and DCs from the location of industries which process primary commodities merges with the general issue of manufacturing for export in LDCs, an issue explored in the following chapter.

---

33.   Wouter Tims, "Possible Effects of Trade Liberalization of Trade in Primary Commodities," (IBRD Staff Working Paper, No. 193.)

34.   See D. Gale Johnson, *World Agriculture in Disarray* (Macmillan, for the Trade Policy Research Centre, 1973).

III. Trade in Manufactures

A. The Generalised System of Preferences (GSP)

The main line pursued by the "Group of 77 non-aligned nations", the LDCs' equivalent to OECD, has been to seek "Special and Differential" treatment for their manufactured exports. The first meeting of UNCTAD .in 1964 put forward the idea that the developed countries should through a Generalised System of Preferences (GSP) eliminate or cut tariffs on all imports of manufactured goods from developing countries while retaining them against other developed countries. Such a policy is clearly discriminatory as between trading partners and runs counter to the basic GATT tenet that tariffs on all trade among its fellow signatories should be subject to exactly the same tariffs as those levied on the "Most Favoured Nation". The only exceptions to that MFN principle, traditionally sanctioned by GATT are customs unions and free trade areas and then only under specified rules.

In terms of economic efficiency, discrimination in trade runs the risk of being "trade diverting", i.e. leading to a shift of the source for imports from relatively low cost exporters to countries with higher relative production costs. The main arguments in favour of the GSP are that equity is more important than efficiency, that this is a reasonable way of giving LDCs more income and that, in any case, many LDCs may have a latent comparative advantage in manufactured goods, but this will only be revealed if they are helped by discrimination to pass through the infant industry stage of manufacturing and marketing for export.

Whether convinced by these arguments, or for other reasons, most of the developed countries have now some form of GSP, usually much diluted versions of the original proposals. Recently, LDCs have shown some alarm at the prospect that general cuts in tariffs in the Tokyo Round MTN will erode their differential advantages gained in the GSP.[35] They have sought extensions in the GSP and opposed the liberal approach of an all round cut in tariffs.

But reliance upon discriminatory treatment in favour of LDCs' manufactured exports has its dangers for LDCs. The tariff concessions have invariably excluded textiles, leather goods and other labour intensive exports of particular interest to LDCs. Moreover, even when tariffs have been abolished quotas or 'voluntary agreements' have imposed quantitative restrictions on

---

35. The general concern is expressed in UNCTAD "The Generalised System of Preferences and MFN Tariff Reduction", (TD/B/C.5/26, Geneva, 1974).

LDCs' exports. Market disruption clauses, subject to the unilateral discretion of the GSP conceding nation, have threatened LDCs with arbitrary and uncertain limitation or loss of markets. Analyses of LDC gains from the GSP have shown them to be fairly small. A recent article by Professors Baldwin and Murray tries to quantify the respective gains likely from the GSP and from general MFN tariff cuts through the GATT Tokyo Round of Trade Negotiations and concludes that they stand to gain more from the latter.[36] But Jaleed Ahmad questions their conclusions in a recent issue of the *Economic Journal.*[37] The conflict over this issue is considered below.

B. The Relative Importance of Exports of Manufactures to LDCs

Agricultural products and minerals remain the largest proportion of the exports of LDCs, but manufactures are now a large and rapidly growing segment of LDCs' exports, particularly when oil is excluded as is shown in Table 2.

The World Bank projects their increase to 55 per cent of non-oil merchandise exports from LDCs, worth $208 billion at 1975 constant prices in 1985. The historical trend rate of growth of these exports is nearly 13 per cent per annum, easily the fastest growing segment of the exports of LDCs (excluding petroleum exports).

Exporting of manufactured goods is still concentrated for the main part on a relatively few countries. Hong Kong, South Korea, Mexico, Brazil, India, Singapore, Malaysia, Argentina, Pakistan and Colombia accounted for 78 per cent of manufactures, other than petroleum products and unworked non-ferrous metals, imported by the industrialised nations from the Third World.[38] But that list includes some of the most populous LDCs. Altogether there are about thirty LDCs which are significant exporters of manufactures. Others are small but growing. It is clear that a continued rapid growth of manufactured exports could bring

---

36. R. E. Baldwin and T. Murray, "MFN tariff reductions and LDC benefits under the GSP", *Economic Journal* (March 1977). See also T. Murray, "How Helpful is the Generalised System of Preference to Developing Countries?" *Economic Journal,* (June 1973).

37. Jaleel Ahmad, "Tokyo Rounds of Trade Negotiations and the Generalised System of Preferences", *The Economic Journal,* (June 1978).

38. Deepak Nayyar, "Transnational Corporations and Manufactured Exports from Poor Countries", *The Economic Journal* (March, 1978) p.61.

Table 2

Composition & Value of LDCs' Non-Oil Merchandise Exports[a]

	1955	1967	1977[b]
	%	%	%
Agricultural Products	76	61	45
Non-Fuel Minerals	13	17	14
Manufactures	10	21	41
Total	100	100	100
Value in US $ Billion	18	28	138
Value in US $(1975) Billion	39	56	107

Notes:
a Excluding capital surplus LDC oil exporting countries.
b Estimated.

Source:
IBRD (World Bank) *Prospects for Developing Countries 1978-85* (November 1977).

substantial benefits to a number of developing countries affecting the lives of many millions of people.

These benefits include increasing the feasible size of industries enabling greater economies of scale, lowering costs, increasing availability of foreign exchange, providing employment opportunities and improving efficiency through the training of labour and management and other external economies. Meeting competition in an export market stimulates efficiency in executives and encourages the acquisition of new ideas, attitudes and skills.

C. Obstacles to LDCs' Manufactured Exports

There are three groups of obstacles to increased exports of manufactures from LDCs:

● LDCs' own commercial policies of restrictions on imports and maintenance of overvalued exchange rates reduce their export competitiveness.

● Barriers to intra LDC trade resulting from their own policies of protection for domestic industries.

● Protection in the industrialised nations, especially quantitative restrictions and tariff escalation.

Many years of import substituting industrialisation behind trade barriers, coupled with the use of exchange restrictions for balance of payments reasons have significantly increased the costs of exportable goods and decreased export incentives. Some countries such as Hong Kong, Singapore and Malaysia have always been relatively free of trade restriction and their exports have done well. Others such as South Korea and Taiwan have also extensively liberalised their trade and used offsetting policies such as high export incentives to counteract distortions. Lately Argentina has started to liberalise. The adverse effects on trade and development of the high levels of protection adopted by most LDCs have been clearly documented in a series of OECD studies.[39] Continuing exchange crises, inefficiency, small scale output, low quality products and technical stagnation have been typical results of high tariffs, quantitative restrictions and over-valued exchange rates. Reduction of these barriers in LDCs where they remain important would contribute significantly to their ability to export manufactures and afford more imports from DCs.

The same prescription holds true for trade with other LDCs. It has grown fastest among the South Asian countries with low trade barriers. But trade among LDCs in manufactures is still smaller than with the rich countries. Moreover, LDCs have much greater difficulties in making adjustments than do richer nations.

The major gains for LDC manufactured exports would be likely to come from reductions in the DC barriers to imports. It is true that by historical standards their tariffs are quite low, under 10 per cent on most finished manufactures. But their highest tariffs generally bear upon labour-intensive manufactures of special interest to LDCs such as clothing, textiles and shoes.

In addition, these same goods are subject to quantitative restrictions (QRs) which are often much more protectionist. The growth of QRs under safeguard and the use of 'Voluntary Export Restrictions' (VERs) and Orderly Marketing Arrangements (OMAs) has borne heavily upon LDCs' manufactured exports, particularly when they were very successful in penetrating foreign markets.

---

39.   I. M. D. Little, T. Scitovsky and M. F. F. Scott, *Industry and Trade in Some Developing Countries: A Comparative Study* (London, Oxford University Press, 1970) summarizes the result of the series of country studies which they organised and edited for OECD.

Finally as tariffs tend to rise at each stage of processing the "effective protection" given to domestic production is normally much higher than the nominal tariff rates.[40] Effective tariffs are well over 30 per cent in many individual products. This hits most severely industries where local value added is low such as wood products, petroleum products and non-ferrous metal processing.

D. The Alternative to the GSP: MFN Tariff Cuts

The main policy issue is whether or not the LDCs should press for deep cuts in tariffs on a MFN basis. Such cuts would reduce their margin of preference under the GSP but the losses from that may be far outweighed by certain advantages of MFN tariff cuts.

- In almost all important exports LDCs face limits upon the volume of their exports which enjoy margins of preference under the GSP. MFN cuts apply to all the goods in the category affected which any country supply.

- Many products of interest to LDCs are excluded from the GSP. MFN tariff cuts would also be subject to exclusions, but the tariff reductions would apply to more goods than fall under the GSP.

- GSP privileges are not available to all LDCs. Some countries are specifically excluded by the GSPs adopted by the largest developed countries. No signatory of the GATT can, under the codes, be excluded from equal treatment in tariffs.

- GSP margins are not guaranteed. They are subject to unilateral withdrawal at any time by the developed country which has extended them. This makes for great uncertainty and is a deterrent to trade. Who would be willing to risk building a factory to export to a specific market if the market can be closed at the whim of the importing nation? MFN tariff reductions are "bound" and cannot be arbitrarily and discriminately altered.

- GSP margins are expected to wither away after a certain time (10 years in the case of the US) but MFN tariff reductions are for an indefinite period.

- An additional psychological or political advantage is that from the viewpoint of producers in the rich nations the giving of preferential margins to some firms and not others is seen as unfair. It is more likely to attract hostility and demands for protection than would MFN tariff reductions.

---

40. See footnote 32.

Many LDC exports are subject to quantitative restrictions and these would be unaffected by MFN cuts, or by maintenance or extension of the GSP. Non-tariff barriers are the subject of separate negotiations in the Multilateral Trade Negotiations. Nevertheless, LDCs would probably be in a stronger position to argue for reduction or removal of such barriers if they were themselves making reciprocal offers to cut their own import barriers. Instead of seeking 'special and differential' treatment they might do much better to make offers and bargain for concessions. Many of their existing tariffs are so high, containing much 'water', that they could be cut in half without significantly increasing their imports. The gesture might be largely empty, but it would be appreciated as a gesture of willingness to be treated as an equal instead of a supplicant.

The calculations of Baldwin and Murray referred to above suggest that the loss of GSP benefits due to a 60 per cent MFN tariff cut would be $32 million. Benefits from MFN tariff cuts would greatly exceed this loss. They amount to $106 million due to absence of value limits, $37 million due to broader product coverage and $268 million due to benefits going to LDCs which are not included in the GSP.[41]

Jaleel Ahmad's main criticism of their results is that they have underestimated the switch to DC exporters from LDC exporters which would occur as a result of the loss of their margin of preference.[42] Clearly this depends upon the elasticity of substitution between DC and LDC exports of similar products. But even if it were much higher than Baldwin and Murray assume, their basic conclusion holds that there would be net positive benefits from the MFN cuts.

But given the relatively low level of most tariffs today they are not too serious a hindrance to LDC exports. Consequently the direct gains from either the GSP or tariff cuts are not very large, less than $500 million per annum. The major gains and losses in trade today are likely to be due to the changes in non-tariff barriers. But the LDCs would, in my view, be in a stronger position to argue against such barriers if they were to abandon the search for 'special and differential' treatment and instead seek equal treatment. The basic

---

41.   Baldwin & Murray, *op. cit.* p.41.

42.   Jaleel Ahmad "Tokyo Rounds of Trade Negotiations and the Generalised System of Preferences" *The Economic Journal,* (June, 1978) p.287.

reality is that most discrimination far from helping the LDC's, actually hurts them. They would suffer most from growing protectionism, and this is the real threat.

As Professor Baldwin puts it:
"The recent trend in protectionism in developed countries is especially frustrating. The European Community (EC) has tightened its quotas on textile imports, while the United States has negotiated orderly marketing agreements (OMA) imposing quantitative controls on exports of shoes from Taiwan and Korea. A similar agreement on colour television sets with Japan is likely to be extended to some developing countries. The agreement between the EC and Japan to limit steel exports from the latter country as well as the possible import restrictions on steel that the United States may negotiate also are likely to apply in the future to developing country exports."[43]

This gives LDCs a strong interest in opposing non-tariff barriers and promoting freer international trade. Their exports of manufactures have been growing fast and are of types which are likely to meet opposition from powerful interests within the developed countries. Large nations like Pakistan, India, Iran, Brazil, Columbia and Mexico have shared in this rapid growth of exports. World Bank and other studies suggest that their capacity to increase supplies is great.[44] The major problem is the reluctance of DCs to open their domestic markets to LDCs' exports. Apart from general protectionist attitudes there are genuine worries about the effects on domestic employment in industries which compete with LDC exports. This involves study of the likely impact on specific industries and regions and of the problems of adjustment involved.

The magnitude of the threat to jobs implied by imports from LDCs is probably exaggerated.[45] Compared with the jobs lost through general recession, faulty macroeconomic policies and

43.   Robert E. Baldwin, "MFN Tariff Reductions Versus Margins of Preferences" (Forthcoming, TPRC, Thames Essay, 1978).

44.   Hollis Chenery and Helen Hughes "Industrialisation and Trade Trends: Some Issues for the 1970s", Chapter 1 in H. Hughes (editor), *Prospects for Partnership,* (World Bank, Washington, 1975), J. M. Finger, *op. cit.* p. 95, G. K. Helleiner, "Manufactured Exports from Less Developed Countries", *Economic Journal* (June 1973).

45.   Caroline Miles, "Employment in the Industrialised Countries", in H. Hughes, *op. cit.* See also I. Little, Scitovsky and Scott, *op. cit., pp. 19-21.*

through technological change the number of workers displaced by imports from LDCs is small. At the same time LDCs are likely to spend any increased earnings of foreign exchange on exports from developed countries. This together with the increased national incomes generated by a better allocation of resources and enhanced competition should ensure that the net effect on jobs is zero or even positive, given time for adjustment. There are three important qualifications to this rather Panglossian view of events:

● The gains are likely to be widely diffused while the losses are apt to be concentrated.

● If the process is sudden, e.g. through a dramatic removal of barriers the adjustment costs could be so immediate and high that they could exceed the value of the future benefits when discounted back to present value terms.

● The effects on individual DCs depend on their relative competitiveness. Some countries may lack confidence in their ability to capture a reasonable share of LDCs' orders for machinery and other goods.

IV. Adjustment Problems of Developed Countries

A. Introduction

The liberal solution normally suggested for this dilemma is adjustment assistance. But there is evidence that in the past much government effort in this field has done little to aid adjustment. Often it has done more to prop up dying industries and provide temporary financial relief to the unemployed. The fears of trade unions that it is largely a failure may be justified. Their concern for the welfare of their members is clearly legitimate and their worries about the fate of their own organisations where these are attached to specific threatened industries are quite understandable. They have been clearly and forcibly expressed by labour leaders Donald Montgomery, Joseph Morris and Jacob Sheinkman in their footnotes to the BNAC Policy Statement in the publication *"The GATT Negotiations 1973-79: The Closing Stage"* by Sidney Golt published in May 1968.

The rapid expansion of manufacturing industry in the LDCs represents both a problem and an opportunity to the DCs. Various developments in the DCs make it clear that continued expansion of their economies depends on structural change. Much of their growth since the Second World War was made possible by a highly elastic supply of labour from agriculture, labour migration and guest workers. These sources of labour have for demographic and social reasons largely dried up. Further progress is dependent on structural change. "The aggregate stability, or decline of the industrial labour force underlines the crucial role of resource mobility between manufacturing branches. The shift of labour from the old, traditional industries to the new and technologically advanced ones, appears to be an eventual prerequisite for future industrial growth."[46]

Resistance to change is one of the forces working for protectionism, additional to the general crisis brought on by inflation, oil crisis, recession, and the unemployment and investment uncertainty created by these events. A recent GATT study stresses the risks involved:

"The spread of protectionist pressures may well prove to be the most important current development in international economic policies, for it has reached a point at which the continued existence of an international order based on agreed and observed rules may be

---

46. U.N., ECE, *Structure and Change in European Industry,* p. XVI (forthcoming publication).

said to be open to question. It is not difficult to identify the sources of the pressures for increased protection. As noted above, between 1973 and 1976 industrial production in developed areas effectively stagnated while in the developing countries industrial capacity, production and exports continued to grow; and in a stagnating market, import-absorption generates additional friction and demands for protection."[47]

Many governments have given way and proliferating barriers to trade through invocation of 'emergency restrictions' and of imposition of so-called 'voluntary export restraints' (VERs), especially on developing countries, have characterised international trade in the last few years. But this widespread resort to trade restrictions implies an "official endorsement of an unwillingness to adjust that is weakening the recovery and growth capacity of the industrial economies."[48] It does so not only by slowing the transfer of resources from less to more productive activities, but also, by casting doubt on the rules of trade, generates uncertainty and slows investment, just when investment is crucially needed to expand aggregate demand and to permit expansion of the more dynamic industries. The growth of protectionism will harm development in both rich and poor countries. There should be strong mutual interest in combating it and continuing the major post-war trends towards freer trade in manufactures.

Most governments admit the long term advantages of free trade. The arguments for British entry into the EEC were largely put in the form of gains from freer trade within Western Europe. But there is a conflict between the perceived long run gains and the risks of painful adjustments. This is a problem. A sudden and unforseen surge in imports may inflict serious hardship on particular industries and especially their workers. The reconciliation of these aspects lies in safeguard measures and in adjustment assistance.

B.   Import Displaced Employment in Perspective

Before considering these two policies, emergency safeguards and adjustment assistance, it would be sensible to try to put the employment problem in perspective. Several recent studies show that quantitatively the threat posed by manufactured imports from

---

47.   GATT, *Prospects for International Trade* (GATT 1196, Sept 1977) p.20.

48.   GATT, *op. cit.* p.21.

developing countries to competing industries in the rich countries is relatively small. The McCraken Report to the OECD stated:
"Imports of manufactures from developing countries were equal to some ¾ per cent of OECD industrial production in 1974 . . . Assuming reasonably open-handed policies on the part of the industrialised countries, their share might rise to 1 ½ to 2 per cent by 1985."[49]

Compared with the effects of labour-saving technological change "the employment-displacement problems created by LDC imports or trade generally are relatively unimportant. In most industrialised countries an annual real growth of 3.4 per cent is necessary to maintain a constant level of overall employment in the face of productivity growth. By contrast, the most recent of a series of studies by the ILO estimated that the employment loss that might be experienced as a result of a total elimination of tariff barriers to LDC imports could be 0.3 per cent of all civil employment in industrialised countries (1.5 per cent of manufacturing employment) spread over a five to ten-year period."[50] Other studies such as R. E. Baldwin's *US Tariff Policy: Formation and Effects* (US Department of Labour Discussion Paper, June 1976) and S. O'Cleireacairn, *"International Trade and Employment in UK Manufacturing: Prospects for the MTN"* (Trade Policy Research Centre, July 1977) confirm that the employment effects of tariff cuts on all imports would be relatively minor. But they all show that the effects would be rather more severe in industries such as footwear and clothing.

Baldwin's study, however, goes on to say that "Not only are the aggregate effects of a significant tariff reduction very small, but the effects on individual industries, on various occupational groups, and on different states (within the USA) are minimal in most cases." (Footwear and Other Leather Products lose 9,150 job man-years between them over the ten years). Earlier work by Little, Scitovsky and Scott and by Caroline Miles produced similar results.[51]

One recent study of American experience in one industry, the Dunlop Report on *The Impact of Imports on the Men's Clothing Industry* in USA (1977) gives a rather high estimate of job losses due

---

49. OECD, *Towards Full Employment and Price Stability* (Paris, June 1977) p.229.

50. ODI Review No. 2 1977, p.30.

51. See Footnote 37 for references.

to imports in suits and coats, shirts and single pants of from 25,000 to 45,000 in the one year 1976. This is, however, based on a very crude model which includes only domestic disposable income and imports as the determinants of employment in those activities. Changes in US exports and the effects of productivity change should surely have been allowed for. It is also rather implausible to assume a stable relationship between disposable income and purchase of clothing during a period of sharp swings in aggregate demand, rapid and changing rates of inflation and high uncertainty.

The weight of the evidence suggests that the reduction of tariff and other barriers to imports of manufactures presents no general threat of unemployment. In fact, the opposite is more likely. The developing countries have a tremendous appetite for manufactures from the OECD nations. Any increased earnings from their exports would be entirely spent on imports which would enable them to operate their economies at higher levels of activity and to grow faster. This increased demand would stimulate employment in the export industries of the OECD nations and permit them to operate their economies at higher levels of activity without the need to depreciate exchange rates. The greater real income generated through a more efficient use of their resources in both DCs and LDCs would also raise aggregate demand.

Even for individual industries, the weight of evidence is that compared with changes in taste and technology, the employment displacing effects of increased imports from developing countries is likely to be minor. A few industries, however, may suffer from time to time real changes in imports which would come too fast to allow normal market forces together with present government policies to produce structural adjustments without imposing real hardship. Likely industries for such problems are clothing, footwear and toys.

A combination of the two policies: (1) use of safeguard procedures and (2) adjustment assistance represents the optimal response to situations of sudden and serious injury inflicted upon a particular domestic industry by a dramatic rise in imports.

C.   Safeguard Procedures

Under the GATT rules the appropriate safeguard procedure is to invoke Article XIX "Emergency Action on Imports of Particular Products". This permits a nation to impose emergency restrictions to enable it to escape temporarily from a tariff concession which it has granted but which because of unforseen developments is causing actual or threatened injury to domestic industry. However, the injury must be serious, due notice must be given and consultation between the interested countries take place before the action is taken ("save where delay would cause damage which it would be difficult to repair"). The affected exporting countries have the right to withdraw equivalent concessions or seek compensation from the country which has harmed them by imposing Article XIX restrictions. Article XIX restrictions must be non-discriminatory as between exporters and they should be lifted as soon as possible.

Article XIX has been used about 80 times and on over half of the occasions it has involved LDC exporters. But more alarming still is that many restrictions have been imposed outside of the GATT rules: either through such arrangements as the Multi-Fibres Agreement or through Voluntary Exports Restrictions and Orderly Marketing Agreements. The need to reform the GATT safeguards procedures has become one of the hottest issues of the Multilateral Trade Negotiations (MTN). The difficulty is to design a safeguards system which gives sufficient latitude to governments to impose restrictions in emergency, that they are encouraged to make faster progress towards relatively free trade, while retaining sufficient disincentives to over-use of escape clauses by governments which bow too easily to pressure from special interest and fail to press ahead with structural adjustments.

Perhaps the major complaint is that too often emergency restrictions have been imposed for periods in excess of five years. A measure intended to give time for adjustment has been used simply as a protective device to avoid adjustment. The use of VERs has often meant that weak, usually developing countries, have had to agree to cut back exports to a country with the political and economic muscle to impose its wishes. As such arrangements are made bilaterally and are 'voluntary' they fall outside the GATT and are not subject to any international surveillance.

There is not the space to spell out the full issues of safeguards reform: I have tried to do this elsewhere.[52] However, the main points that should be included in a safeguards procedure are:

● Retention of the rule of non-discrimination; because without this the weaker nations will suffer discrimination.
● Objective assessment of injury and of the required duration of

---

52.   Alasdair MacBean, "How to Repair the 'Safety Net' of the International Trading System", *The World Economy,* Trade Policy Research Centre, December, 1977.

the safeguards through international surveillance, with some arrangements for putting pressure on nations to make structural adjustments.

● No requirements for compensation nor resort to retaliation without agreement in an international panel that the country which invoked the restrictions did so needlessly.

D.   Adjustment Assistance

But the main response of nations to increased imports should be to aid structural adjustment. To do this properly requires that procedures be agreed in advance and that industries likely to face difficulties are identified before the problems become severe, fester and stimulate demands for protection. Many governments do have devices for adjustment assistance, but there is evidence that up to now most of their endeavours in this field have done little to aid structural adjustment in the face of increased imports.

The general conclusions of an OECD study are worth presenting:[53]

● The displacement effect of imports from developing countries has been minimal when seen in relation to the magnitude of total structural change in industrialised countries.

● No industrialised countries have so far pursued adjustment assistance policies specifically designed to promote imports from developing countries although a few attempts have been made to accelerate the contraction of individual sectors.

● More often, however, public policy had sought to delay the transfer of resources. *The greatest contribution to rapid re-allocation has probably been the pursuit of full employment and a generally high level of demand.*

● The pursuit of an improved international division of labour is not a matter merely of trade policy and trade-focussed adjustment measures. Developed countries must direct their attention to the whole complex of structural, regional and employment policies in their countries. If these policies are to promote rather than thwart the expansion of exports from developing countries they must not remain politically and administratively isolated from trade policy.

Outlines of the existing adjustment assistance measures in use in the main industrialised nations are available in that OECD study

---

53.   OECD Development Centre, *Adjustment for Trade: Studies in Industrial Adjustment Problems* (Paris 1975), p.11.

and in an UNCTAD Report published in May 1977.[54] Between them these two studies cover the measures used in Belgium, Canada, Germany, Netherlands, Japan, Sweden, the UK and USA.

What emerges from these studies is that apart from the Netherlands and USA no country has used measures specifically designed to facilitate trade liberalisation. In particular their policies have not been intended to foster the expansion of imports of manufactures from developing countries, nor to encourage the redeployment to developing countries of industries which have ceased to be competitive on their own. But in some countries, for example Canada, the policies and programmes are sufficiently flexible to be used for these objectives.

In most countries there is a range of measures designed to meet social and economic objectives arising from structural and demographic change. Some of these have effects which run counter to structural adaptation to new circumstances. For example, regional policies to reduce unemployment may have the effect of shoring up obsolescent industries. This has also been true of certain types of trade adjustment policies. Loans to firms which have been hard hit by imports may be used to purchase more modern equipment in what may be a vain bid to become competitive once more.

E. Basic Requirements for Adjustment Assistance

Motives for providing assistance to enable industry and workers to adjust to increased imports fall into two categories. These are:

- To reduce suffering, prevent waste of resources through unemployment and underutilisation of industrial capacity, and to facilitate structural change, and
- To buy off potential lobbyists for protection.

The first of these motives has very little to do with imports. Any change in pattern of demand, in aggregate demand, in labour saving innovations, in exchange rates, in foreign demand for exports, or in various government policies with regard to taxes, subsidies and nationalised industries can cause unemployment. Why should one give special assistance for one type of hazard when there are so many? Equally, in so far as any change is long term it would involve structural change. Such change will often be resisted by those

---

54.   UNCTAD Adjustment Assistance Measures, TD/B/C.2/171 Geneva, 27 May 1977 and TD/121/Supp. 1. 14 January 1972.

directly affected and adjustment is one way of reducing this resistance. The argument for special treatment for those workers (and businessmen) whose adjustment problems arise mainly from increases in imports has to hang on the second aim of reducing the pressure for protection.

It has to be recognised that the threat from "cheap imports" arouses primitive nationalism in many breasts. The pressure to change stemming from this source is generally more strongly resisted than change originating in labour displacing technology or changes in fashion. But it is particularly damaging to economic progress if it is permitted to do so. Not only does protection hold up economic changes which are probably inevitable, but it provokes retaliation or immitation by other countries, threatening the liberal international economic order which has fostered great economic progress over the lasm 30 years. Accordingly effective adjustment policies tied to the specific problem of industry displacing imports may now be a *sine qua non* for maintenance and development of free international trade. This certainly appears to be the case in USA from the 1962 Trade Expansion Act onwards, and if the growth of protectionist forces there and elsewhere is to be resisted successfully adjustment assistance must be made to work. All this is despite the long list of careful studies which show that, objectively reduction of barriers to LDC manufactured exports is a minor cause of jobs displacement compared with the other major causes.

One implication of the foregoing is that even if in legislation one has to make a distinction between problems caused by import penetration and those due to other causes, eligibility for assistance should not be interpreted strictly. The significant criterion for assistance should be whether the activity is obsolescent and the firms and workers can be helped to move to more promising activities.

The attempt of the US Trade Expansion Act (TEA) to define eligibility too precisely seriously reduced its usefulness. Appellants were required to demonstrate:
- That competing imports had been increasing;
- That a tariff concession was the major reason for the increase; and
- That increased imports were a major cause of injury to the domestic industry.

Rigorous requirements of this sort brought Charles Frank's condemnation of the TEA measures as 'a cumbersome and ineffective form of adjustment assistance . . . the criteria for eligibility are so strict that only the very sickest, most poorly managed, and most unfortunate firms are declared eligible'.[55] No wonder some labour leaders called it 'burial assistance'.

Adjustment assistance involves help both to workers and to firms.[56] But the problem of unemployment of labour is the main cause for concern. It is particularly difficult when the industry is concentrated in a particular area and is much tougher where there is general unemployment and slow growth in the economy. In the 1950s and '60s contraction of the textile industries caused little difficulty as workers moved freely and willingly from these low wage occupations to better paid employment in expanding industries. Now with slow growth and high average levels of unemployment adjustment assistance is much more necessary.

While unemployment of labour is the major problem, underutilisation of plant and machinery can also be a significant social loss. This is not so if the industry cannot sell the products from its specialised equipment at a profit. The value of a machine is the net present value of the future stream of earnings from it plus any scrap value. If it can earn no profits its only value is as scrap. In this situation there is no social loss from its underutilisation. But if it could be made to pay, say by rationalisation of the industry, this would justify assistance to keep going while some firms withdraw from the industry.

F.   Types of Assistance

1.   *To workers*

Workers made redundant most of all need income support. In most OECD nations unemployment insurance benefit and redundancy payments may already be adequate but to make adjustment more acceptable it is probably advisable to pay additional compensation to workers where import competition has been a factor in their loss of employment. Older workers who may be confronted with greater difficulties in finding alternative employment and suffer more shock from sudden redundancy, have a special case for additional cash grants.

Secondly, they need opportunities to learn new skills. This need not be through formal retraining programmes though those may

---

55.   *OECD op. cit.* p. 237.

56.   The following six paragraphs lean heavily on Caroline Miles, "Introduction to the OECD Study *Adjustment for Trade*.".

also be valuable. Grants enabling workers to finance their own retraining may work as well. Such survey evidence as there is does not show very high returns from government training programmes. They may be too inflexible or trainees may merely take jobs from others.[57] Relocation costs could also be met from adjustment assistance if other sources do not provide this.

2.   *To firms*

The objective is to encourage enterprises which have long term viability and to help firms to move out of activities which are already, or soon will be uneconomic. This does not always mean moving out of the industry. A great deal of the growth in trade nowadays is intra-industry rather than inter-industry. This is partly because industry labels are rather broad and encompass within them many very different activities. Product differentiation, economies of scale, fashion and variety in the available production technologies among other factors, make it quite common for countries to export and import rather similar goods at the same time.

Where firms are non-viable the need is to eliminate them from the industry as painlessly as possible. The generally accepted method is to subsidise the scrapping of plant.

Re-equipment is a more difficult issue. Where firms can be viable with a little help, equipment grants or loans can be justified, for even good firms may find it difficult to attract capital in a declining industry which has a 'bad name'. But it is difficult to discriminate in advance as between those firms which have a good future and those which have not. There is a risk that the wrong ones will gain resources and that the adjustment problem is merely prolonged. There are always arguments ready to hand which can be used to gain government aid to prop up sections of industries which should have been encouraged to adjust. Examples from shipbuilding, steel, motorcycles and automobiles in the UK are not hard to find.

One can try to safeguard against this by ensuring objective scrutiny by an independent body. Caroline Miles recommends an investment bank type of institution for this purpose.

G.   Some Policy Suggestions

  ● There is a need to develop an early warning system so that industries at risk can be identified and measures set on foot so that

---

57.   Goran Ohlin, "Adjustment Assistance in Sweden" OECD *op. cit.* p. 208.

costs of adjustment can be minimised and protectionist forces do not have time to build up.

● Adjustment policies should be linked to Safeguard Procedures. When a country seeks permission to use emergency restrictions it should be required to show that it is taking action to promote structural adjustment.

● Adjustment assistance with respect to imports cannot be considered in isolation from the whole complex of general, regional, sectoral and social policies. They have to be harmonised lest they work against adjustment.

● There may be a need in some cases to set up special government agencies to carry out the policies. Government departments each have their own axes to grind and may be too close to the short term whims of their political masters. Semi-autonomous bodies could take a broader and longer view of the nations' interests in structural adjustment without the same pressure from politicians with import sensitive constituencies. However, the issues are probably too politically sensitive for governments ever to let them out of their direct control.

V. The Special Problem of the Least Developed Countries

It can be expected that most of the benefits from the proposals outlined above would tend to go the the more advanced LDCs. Certainly for some considerable time the gains from increased exports of manufactures will accrue mainly to South East Asian countries, Brazil, Mexico and some other Latin American nations, India and Pakistan. Most manufacturing investment and transfers of technology by the transnational corporations are also likely to take place in the countries which already have reasonable infrastructure and existing industries. To counter-balance this bias special measures may have to be taken in favour of the least developed among the developing countries.

This view has certainly been expressed in UNCTAD Resolution 98(iv) which sets out special measures to be taken in favour of that special group "the least developed countries". They are distinguished on the basis of three characteristics: per capita GDP, share of manufacturing in GDP and the proportion of literate persons over the age of fifteen in the population. There is a substantial element of arbitrariness in the classification because of the poor quality of the available statistics. But setting that aside they form a group of very poor countries mostly in Central Africa. Bangladesh, Tanzania and the Democratic Yemen are the other major countries included.

The UNCTAD recommended that twenty five countries, categorised as least developed countries, should receive an increased proportion of a larger aid flow and more technical assistance. Aid should be mainly on a grant basis and their official debts should be cancelled. The criteria used for project aid should take greater account of secondary benefits and of longer term gains.

In the field of commercial policy they are to be given special consideration in commodity agreements (but in such a way that this does not harm other members' interests) in the GSP and in the IMF's Compensatory Financing Facility, in help with setting up processing industries and generally in the multilateral trade negotiation and in the integrated programme for commodities. There are other recommendations, but they are much less central to the task of developed nations helping the least developed countries.[58]

---

58. UNCTAD TD/191 (1976) and UNCTAD Resolution 98 (iv), (28th June 1976) give a full list of views and recommendations. Pp. 45-48 of this paper draw on my earlier paper "The Economic Situation of the Least Developed Countries" presented to the conference on a NIEO in New Delhi, (December 1977).

More of everything for the least developed means less for the other developing countries. The UNCTAD proposals try to dodge the issue, but fail to do so. A larger quota for their exports in an ICA must mean smaller quotas for others if the same target price is to be maintained. More financial aid for them will mean less for others. But as many of the others are just as poor and certainly several contain far greater numbers of the poorest people in the world, the morality of the action is unclear. Why should resources be diverted from such countries as India, Pakistan, Egypt or Thailand to this fairly arbitrarily chosen group? It would carry more moral authority if aid agencies and trading nations were simply urged to bear in mind the interests of the poorest people in the world when deciding policies. But they also have to consider the effectiveness with which the resources are likely to be used.

The aid proposals are unhelpful. To lower the criteria for acceptance of projects means lowering the average productivity of aid in general. It is quite a different matter to include within the criteria some extra weight to be attributed to benefits going to poorer people. The World Bank and other aid agencies already do this as well as taking into account external benefits and costs in project evaluation. More technical assistance sounds splendid but in fact the least developed countries are already receiving a higher than average amount of technical assistance. Donors already do a great deal to devise and implement programmes in these countries. Perhaps in the past they have done too much. Western aid agencies bear a considerable part of the responsibility for the Sahelian disaster, through ill-thought out interventions in the supply of artesian wells and veterinary assistance.[59]

The absorptive capacity for aid is often low in these countries. Unstable governments, weak administration and lack of skilled people makes it difficult to find good projects. There is an absorptive capacity limit for TA as well as for financial aid. There are political limits to the number of foreigners who are welcome in high positions and there is a shortage of people sufficiently educated to be counterparts of TA personnel.

The suggestions of cancellation of debt, while politically

---

59.   This judgement is based on my reading of French and US AID official analyses of the problems of the Sahele when I was on an AID Mission in Chad. But similar old policy errors are documented in William and Elizabeth Paddock, *We Don't Know How* (Iowa State Univ. Press/Ames, 1973).

appealing are disingenuous. Most aid budgets are planned in terms of net disbursements. This is how they are reported to OECD. If the flow of repayments is reduced that means less money is available for new lending. Some recipients of aid must lose out and they may be more deserving than those whose debts have been cancelled.

There is one area of assistance which generally does not require much local skilled help and that is exploration for ground water, design of irrigation schemes, evaluation of soil conditions for agriculture, and exploration for minerals. In many of these countries there is a serious lack of knowledge of their basic natural resource endowment. The UNDP has considerable experience in organising such pre-investment survey work and the multinational corporations would no doubt come in if the political risks were taken care of and the terms were attractive. Progress in these areas would seem feasible and the potential benefits are high.

It is unlikely that commodity agreements would bring much to these countries. A coffee agreement which raised coffee prices would bring some benefits but we have already shown how difficult this is. Cotton, textile fabrics, oil seeds and jute are most unlikely to have their prices raised by ICAs because of the risks of substitution. Petroleum and natural gas are exported by some of them and these products are likely to continue to do well without ICAs. Intervention to raise prices in such diverse products as hides and skins or fruits and nuts seems out of the question. But that list covers almost all their current exports.

They would gain far more from reduced barriers to their exports, especially those which compete with temperate zone agricultural products. Many of the African countries can produce high quality meat and have potential for large scale cattle ranching and with irrigation, grain production. They could gain from increased exports of sugar, meat, oil seeds and fruit if barriers were reduced.

The problem of speeding development in backward, relatively isolated countries is not amenable to swift or dramatic solution. The answer does not lie in massive intervention by the West. Their progress will take time. They can be helped in various ways suggested above, but for many years the fruits of this will be marginal and there will almost certainly continue to be a need for emergency relief when drought or other disaster strikes countries which have no reserves. This constitutes one additional argument for stocks of grain held either internationally or by the big grain nations. Although the merits of ICAs in general are unconvincing the potential benefits from grain reserves, in terms of avoiding famine, are so high that the world can well afford the costs of maintaining them.[60]

---

60.   D. Gale Johnson, "Limitations of Grain Reserves in the Quest for stable prices", *The World Economy* (June 1978). See also Timothy Josling, "An International Grain Reserve Policy", BNAC, 1973.

VI. Conclusions on the Trade Issues

In almost every aspect of international trade the greatest harm that can befall the developing countries as a whole is an increase in protectionism both in the rich nations and in their own economies. The existing interventions in trade already severely damage their interests. In the commodity field the protection of agriculture in almost all of the industrialised nations reduces both the price and volume of their agricultural exports. The form which protection normally takes, quantitative restrictions and variable import levies, has a significantly destabilising impact on the international prices of many primary commodities. Those manufactured exports in which developing countries have the greatest comparative advantage are frustrated by the quotas imposed under the Multi Fibre Agreement, VERs, OMAs and other "illegal" measures.

The developing countries are apt to be seen by industries in the industrialised nations as the disrupters, the newcomers whose exports cost them profits and jobs. As most of the LDCs are relatively small and with little bargaining power individually they are most likely to be the victim of any changes in the international economic order which make it even easier for the rich nations to discriminate against them. The LDCs should be in the forefront of those who seek the maintenance and strengthening of the 'rule of law' as embodied in the GATT charter and codes. Freer international trade in commodities, semi-processed goods and manufactures would bring them great benefits. This is the 'first best' solution to their problems. As long as there is a chance of averting increased protection and of lowering some of the barriers to their exports they should fight within the GATT and UNCTAD for these objectives. Not only could success there bring direct benefits in terms of better prices and larger volumes of exports, it would help the rich nations to recover from their present recession and stagflation. That in itself would do more to raise LDC export earnings than any other conceivable measure.

Only if there is no possibility of making any progress in liberalising trade should the LDCs take up the much inferior 'second or third' best policies of attempts at market intervention and control through commodity agreements, export taxes and the GSP. Even then it is doubtful if they could improve their trade situation much through these strategems.

The rich nations, both in their own long term interests and for the sake of equity should reduce their barriers to LDCs' exports, and adjust their own economies by shifting resources to higher productivity, higher wage activities. In general the problem of adjustment without hardship to increased imports should not be too difficult. In most industries the number of jobs lost in any year will be tiny in relation to the normal turnover of workers in these industries. But in a few cases the pace of adjustment may be too high to be left to market forces. Then the state must intervene, preferably with adjustment assistance measures and generous compensation for displaced workers, but if necessary through use of Article XIX safeguard measures to restrict desrupting imports temporarily.

Appendix A

BUFFER STOCKS EFFECT ON PRICES: A TECHNICAL NOTE

The effect of the actions of a buffer stock in stabilising price can be analysed in terms of a simple diagram with linear supply and demand functions and random shifts in either supply or demand. Where the cause of instability is shifts in supply and the price elasticity of demand is greater than 0.5 the effect of price stabilisation is: (a) to destabilise total earnings as compared with a free market (b) to increase the average level of producers earnings over boom and slump as compared with a free market. (See Fig. 1)

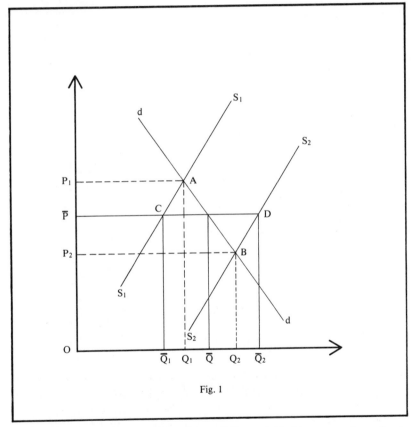

Fig. 1

(a) 1. When supply increases from OQ_1 to OQ_2 this causes the price to decrease from OP_1 to OP_2. Although price has fallen substantially, revenue has changed much less: from OP_1AQ_1 to OP_2BQ_2.

2. When the price is held constant at $\bar{P}$ producers receive $O\bar{P}C\bar{Q}$, when supply is S_1. The buffer stock releases $\bar{Q}\bar{Q}_1$ from stock. When supply is S_2 the producers receive $O\bar{P}D\bar{Q}_2$ and the buffer stock buys $\bar{Q}Q_2$ from the

market. The ratio $O\bar{P}D\bar{Q}_2/O\bar{P}C\bar{Q}_1$ is clearly much greater than OP_2BQ_2/OP_1AQ_1.

(b) However, the sum of $O\bar{P}D\bar{Q}_2$ plus $O\bar{P}C\bar{Q}_1$ is greater than the sum of OP_2BQ_2 plus OP_1AQ_1.

The converse is true in a demand shift market. In this case stabilising the price will (i) stabilise revenue, but will (ii) reduce average revenue over the cycle. (Fig. 2).

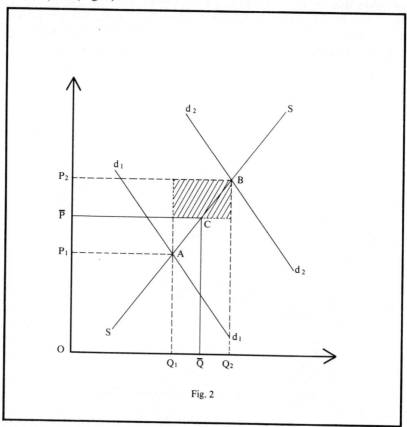

Fig. 2

(a) Clearly when price is stabilised at $\bar{P}$ in this case revenue remains $O\bar{P}C\bar{Q}$ in both boom and slump, whereas it fluctuates considerably if price is left free.

(b) When earnings are summed over both periods they become twice $O\bar{P}C\bar{Q}$ with the buffer stock operating to hold price at $\bar{P}$, and OP_1AQ_1 + OP_2BQ_2 when the market is free. But the latter sum exceeds the former by the shaded rectangle at B.

My colleague Tin Nguyen has reworked these possibilities using non-linear functions and allowing both supply and demand to shift randomly at the same time. His conclusions are that price stabilisation (a) stabilises revenue if market instability is largely *demand-induced* and (b) destabilises revenue if *either* (i) market instability is caused equally by supply and demand shifts and demand is price elastic *or* (ii) market instability is largely *supply-induced* and price elasticity of demand exceeds a *half* (or a lower value still if price elasticity of supply is positive). Price stabilisation is shown to have *no effect* on the long-term *level* of revenue if the supply and demand shifts have log normal distributions.*

---

*D. T. Nguyen, "The Implications of Price Stabilisation for the Short-Term Instability and Long-Term Level of LDCs' Export Earnings" forthcoming in *The Quarterly Journal of Economics (1979)*.

Appendix B

THE VALUE AND SHARE OF WORLD TRADE IN COMMODITIES OF DEVELOPING COUNTRIES

Table B1
The Value and Share of World Exports of Developing Countries for Eighteen Commodities.

	Value of Exports (US $ million)	Per cent of World Exports
10 'core' Commodities		
Coffee	$3,052	84.6%
Tea	626	78.8
Cocoa	1,247	84.7
Sugar	4,040	70.7
Rubber	1,428	97.5
Jute Fibre	184	96.8
Jute manufactures	462	92.0
Hard Fibres	160	100.0
Hard Fibre manufactures	69	100.0
Cotton Fibre	2,165	71.2
Cotton yarn	369	44.9
Copper	2,881	48.6
Tin	838	80.9
Total	**$17,521**	**69.9%**
8 'other' Commodities		
Manganese	$184	69.2%
Rock phosphates	558	51.3
Iron ore	1,317	37.8
Bauxite	258	71.1
Non-coniferous timber	1,203	52.7
Vegetable oils	1,322	45.8
Vegetable oilseeds	959	24.7
Meat	1,095	16.2
Bananas	536	90.5
Total	**$7,432**	**34.4%**
Total 18 Commodities	**$24,953**	**53.5%**

Source: Commonwealth Secretariat

Table B2
Share of Developed and Developing Countries
in the Total World Trade of Eighteen Commodities

	Trade Share in 10 'core' Commodities[a]	Trade Share in 18 Commodities[a]
Developed Countries Total	44.8%	58.5%
p.c. income in 1973:		
(1) above $4,000 p.a.	26.7	34.5
(2) below $4,000 p.a.	18.1	24.0
Developing Countries Total	40.5	30.8
(1) major petroleum exporters	4.1	3.2
(2) fast growing exporters of manufactures	2.0	2.0
(3) other countries with p.c. income in 1973 above $400 p.a.	19.8	14.9
(4) countries with p.c. income in 1973 between $200—$400 p.a.	7.1	5.7
(5) countries with p.c. income in 1973 below $200 p.a. (Excluding "hard core" least developed countries)	4.8	3.2
(6) "hard core" least developed countries	2.7	1.8
Centrally Planned Economics: Total	14.7	10.7
Total	100.0%	100.0%

Notes:

a — Average of combined import and export values in 1970-5.

p.c. — per capita.

p.a. — per annum

Source: Commonwealth Secretariat

Appendix C

RESOLUTION ADOPTED BY THE UNITED NATIONS CONFERENCE ON TRADE AND DEVELOPMENT FOURTH SESSION, NAIROBI, MAY 1976

93 (IV) Integrated Programme for Commodities

The United Nations Conference on Trade and Development,

Recalling the Declaration and the Programme of Action on the Establishment of a New International Economic Order as well as the Charter of Economic Rights and Duties of States, which lay down the foundations of the new international economic order, General Assembly resolution 623 (VII) of 21 December 1952 and Conference recommendateon A.11.1,

Recalling, in particular, section 1, paragraph 3(a)(iv), of the Programme of Action on the Establishment of a New International Economic Order, relating to the preparation of an overall integrated programme for 'a comprehensive range of commodities of export interest to developing countries',

Recalling also Section I, paragraph 3, of General Assembly resolution 3362 (S-VII) of 16 September 1975, which states, *inter alia,* that 'an important aim of the fourth session of the United Nations Conference on Trade and Development, in addition to work in progress elsewhere, should be to reach decisions on the improvement of market structures in the field of raw materials, and commodities of export interest to the developing countries, including decisions with respect to an integrated programme and the applicability of elements thereof'.

Taking note of the work undertaken on commodities in preparation for the fourth session of the Conference, in particular the proposals submitted by the Secretary-General of UNCTAD for an integrated programme for commodities,

Reaffirming the important role of UNCTAD in the field of commodities,

Bearing in mind resolution 16 (VIII) of the Committee on Commodities concerning decisions by the Conference at its fourth session with respect to an integrated programme for commodities, on, *inter alia:*

(a) objectives;
(b) commodities to be covered;
(c) international measures;
(d) follow-up procedures and time-table for the implementation of agreed measures;

Affirming the importance to both producers and consumers, notably the developing countries, of commodity exports for foreign exchange earnings and of commodity imports for welfare and economic development,

Recognizing the need to conduct international trade on the basis of mutual advantage and equitable benefits, taking into account the interests of all States, particularly those of the developing countries,

Recognizing also the need for improved forms of international co-operation in the field of commodities which should promote economic and social development, particularly of the developing countries,

Recognizing further the urgent need for substantial progress in stimulating food production in developing countries and the important bearing of international commodity policies on this aim,

Recalling the proposal in the Manila Declaration and Programme of Action for the establishment of a common fund for the financing of international commodity stocks, co-ordinated national stocks or other necessary measures within the framework of commodity arrangements,

Bearing in mind the view that there might be financial savings in operating a central facility for the purpose of financing buffer stocks,

Taking note of the readiness of a number of countries, expressed prior to and at the fourth session of the Conference, to participate in and financially support a common fund,

Noting that there are differences of views as to the objectives and modalities of a common fund,

Convinced of the need for an overall approach and an integrated programme for commodities which is a programme of global action to improve market structures in international trade in commodities of interest to developing countries, and which is consistent with the interests of all countries, particularly those of the developing countries, and assures a comprehensive view of the various elements involved while respecting the characteristics of individual commodities.'

Decides to adopt the following Integrated Programme for Commodities:

I. Objectives

With a view to improving the terms of trade of developing countries and in order to eliminate the economic imbalance between developed and developing countries, concerted efforts should be made in favour of the developing countries towards expanding and diversifying their trade, improving and diversifying their productive capacity, improving their productivity and increasing their export earnings, with a view to counteracting the adverse effects of inflation, thereby sustaining real incomes. Accordingly the following objectives are agreed:

1. To achieve stable conditions in commodity trade, including avoidance of excessive price fluctuations, at levels which would:
   (a) be remunerative and just to producers and equitable to consumers;
   (b) take account of world inflation and changes in the world economic and monetary situations;
   (c) promote equilibrium between supply and demand within expanding world commodity trade;
2. To improve and sustain the real income of individual developing countries through increased export earnings, and to protect them from fluctuations in export earnings, especially from commodities;
3. To seek to improve market access and reliability of supply for

primary products and the processed products thereof, bearing in mind the needs and interests of developing countries;

4. To diversify production in developing countries, including food production, and to expand processing of primary products in developing countries with a view to promoting their industrialization and increasing their export earnings;

5. To improve the competitiveness of, and to encourage research and development on the problems of, natural products competing with synthetics and substitutes, and to consider the harmonization, where appropriate, of the production of synthetics and substitutes in developed countries with the supply of natural products produced in developing countries;

6. To improve market structures in the field of raw materials and commodities of export interest to developing countries;

7. To improve marketing, distribution and transport system for commodity exports of developing countries, including an increase in their participation in these activities and their earnings from them.

II.   Commodity Coverage

The commodity coverage of the Integrated Programme should take into account the interests of developing countries in bananas, bauxite, cocoa, coffee, copper, cotton and cotton yarns, hard fibres and products, iron ore, jute and products, manganese, meat, phosphates, rubber, sugar, tea, tropical timber, tin, and vegetable oils, including olive oil, and oilseeds, among others, it being understood that other products could be included, in accordance with the procedure set out in section IV below.

III.   International Measures of the Programme

1. It is agreed that steps will be taken, as described in section IV, paragraphs 1 to 3 below, towards the negotiation of a common fund.

2. It is also agreed to take the following measures, to be applied singly or in combination, including action in the context of international commmodity arrangements between products and consumers, in the light of the characteristics and problems of each commodity and the special needs of developing countries;

(a) Setting up of international commodity stocking arrangements;

(b) Harmonization of stocking policies and the setting up of co-ordinated national stocks;

(c) Establishment of pricing arrangements, in particular negotiated price ranges, which would be periodically reviewed and appropriately revised, taking into account, *inter alia,* movements in prices of imported manufactured goods, exchange rates, production costs and world inflation, and levels of production and consumption;

(d) Internationally agreed supply management measures, including export quotas and production policies and, where appropriate,

multilateral long-term supply and purchase commitments;
(e) Improvements of procedures for information and consultation on market conditions;
(f) Improvement and enlargement of compensatory financing facilities for the stabilization, around a growing trend, of export earnings of developing countries;
(g) Improvement of market access for the primary and processed products of developing countries through multilateral trade measures in the multilateral trade negotiations, improvement of schemes of generalised preferences and their extension beyond the period originally envisaged, and trade promotion measures;
(h) International measures to improve the infrastructure and industrial capacity of developing countries, extending from the production of primary commodities to their processing, transport and marketing, as well as to the production of finished manufactured goods, their transport, distribution and exchange, including the establishment of financial, exchange and other institutions for the remunerative management of trade transactions;
(i) Measures to encourage research and development on the problems of natural products competing with synthetics and consideration of the harmonization where appropriate, of the production of synthetics and substitutes in developed countries with the supply of natural products produced in developing countries;
(j) Consideration of special measures for commodities whose problems cannot be adequately solved by stocking and which experience a persistent price decline.

3. The interests of developing importing countries, particularly the least developed and the most seriously affected among them, and those lacking in natural resources, adversely affected by measures under the Integrated Programme, should be protected by means of appropriate differential and remedial measures within the Programme.
(i) Measures to encourage research and development on the problems of natural products competing with synthetics and consideration of the harmonization where appropriate, of the production of synthetics and substitutes in developed countries with the supply of natural products produced in developing countries;
(j) Consideration of special measures for commodities whose problems cannot be adequately solved by stocking and which experience a persistent price decline.

3. The interests of developing importing countries, particularly the least developed and the most seriously affected among them, and those lacking in natural resources, adversely affected by measures under the Integrated Programme, should be protected by means of appropriate differential and

remedial measures within the Programme.

4.   Special measures, including exemption from financial contribution, should be taken to accommodate the needs of the least developed countries in the Integrated Programme for Commodities.

5.   Efforts on specific measures for reaching arrangements on products, groups of products or sectors which, for various reasons, are not incorporated in the first stage of application of the Integrated Programme should be continued.

6.   The application of any of the measures which may concern existing international arrangements on commodities covered by the Integrated Programme would be decided by governments within the commodity organizations concerned.

IV.   Procedures and Time Table

1.   The Secretary-General of UNCTAD is requested to convene a negotiating conference open to all members of UNCTAD on a common fund no later than March 1977.

2.   The Secretary-General of UNCTAD is further requested to convene preparatory meetings prior to the conference referred to in paragraph 1 above concerning, *inter alia:*

(a)   Elaboration of objectives;

(b)   The financing needs of a common fund and its structure;

(c)   Sources of finance;

(d)   Mode of operations;

(e)   Decision-making and fund management.

3.   Member countries are invited to transmit to the Secretary-General of UNCTAD, prior to 30 September 1976, any proposals they may have concerning the above and related issues.

4.   The Secretary-General of UNCTAD is further requested to convene, in consultation with international organizations concerned, preparatory meetings for international negotiations on individual products, in the period beginning 1 September 1976. These meetings should complete their work as soon as possible, but not later than February 1978. The task of the preparatory meetings shall be to:

(a)   Propose appropriate measures and techniques required to achieve the objectives of the Integrated Programme;

(b)   **Determine financial requirements resulting from the measures and techniques proposed;**

(c)   Recommend follow-up action required through the negotiation of commodity agreements, or other measures;

(d)   Prepare draft proposals of such agreements for the consideration of governments and for use in commodity negotiating conferences.

5.   The Secretary-General of UNCTAD is further requested to convene, as and when required, commodity negotiating conferences as soon as

possible after the completion of each preparatory meeting held pursuant to paragraph 4 above. These negotiations should be concluded by the end of 1978.

6. The Secretary-General of UNCTAD is requested to undertake the necessary arrangements for the servicing of the preparatory meetings and the subsequent commodity negotiating conferences, in co-operation with the secretariats of the specialized commodity bodies and other organizations concerned.

7. It is agreed that international negotiations or re-negotiations on individual commodities covered by existing agreements shall be in accordance with appropriate established procedure for the purpose of concluding international arrangements.

8. The Trade and Development Board is instructed to establish an *ad hoc* inter-governmental committee to co-ordinate the preparatory work and the negotiations, to deal with major policy issues that may arise, including commodity coverage, and to co-ordinate the implementation of the measures under the Integrated Programme.

Members of the
British-North American Committee

AUGUSTIN S. HART, JR.
Vice Chairman, Quaker Oats
Company, Chicago, Illinois

G. R. HEFFERNAN
President,
Co-Steel International Limited,
Whitby, Ontario

HENRY J. HEINZ II
Chairman of the Board, H. J. Heinz
Company, Pittsburgh, Pennsylvania

ROBERT HENDERSON
Chairman,
Kleinwort Benson Ltd., London

ROBERT P. HENDERSON
President and Chief
Executive Officer, Itek
Corporation, Lexington,
Massachusetts

JACK HENDLEY
General Manager (International),
Midland Bank Limited, London

WILLIAM R. HEWLETT
President and Chief Executive,
Hewlett-Packard Company,
Palo Alto, California

HENDRIK S. HOUTHHAKKER
Professor of Economics,
Harvard University,
Cambridge, Massachusetts

TOM JACKSON
General Secretary, Union of Post
Office Workers, Clapham, London

DEAN DONALD JACOBS
Graduate School of Managment
Evanston, Illinois

JOHN V. JAMES
President and Chief Executive Officer,
Dresser Industries, Dallas, Texas

GEORGE S. JOHNSTON
President, Scudder, Stevens & Clark,
New York, New York

JOSEPH D. KEENAN
President, Union Label and Service
Trades Department, AFL-CIO,
Washington, D.C.

TOM KILLEFER
President, United States Trust
Company of New York, New York

LANE KIRKLAND
Secretary-Treasurer,
AFL-CIO, Washington, D.C.

CURTIS M. KLAERNER
Executive Vice President and Director,
Mobil Oil Corporation, New York,
New York

H. U. A. LAMBERT
Vice Chairman, Barclays Bank Limited,
London

HERBERT H. LANK
Director, Du Pont of Canada Ltd.,
Montreal, Quebec

WILLIAM A. LIFFERS
Vice Chairman,
American Cyanamid Company,
Wayne, New Jersey

JAY LOVESTONE
International Affairs Consultant,
AFL-CIO, Washington, D.C.

RAY W. MACDONALD
Honorary Chairman,
Burroughs Corporation,
Detroit, Michigan

CARGILL MacMILLAN, JR.
Senior Vice President, Cargill
Incorporated, Minneapolis, Minnesota

Sponsoring Organisations

The British-North American Research Association was inaugurated in December 1969 as an independent, non-profit making organization. Its primary purpose is to sponsor research on British-North American economic relations in association with the British-North American Committee. Publications of the British-North American Research Association as well as publications of the British-North American Committee are available at the association's office, 1 Gough Square, London EC4A 3DE (Tel: 01-353 6371).

The Association is a registered educational charity and is governed by a council under the chairmanship of Sir Richard Dobson.

The National Planning Association is an independent, private, non-profit, non-political organization that carries on research and policy formulation in the public interest. NPA was founded during the Great Depression of the 1930s when conflicts among the major economic groups—business, farmers, labour—threatened to paralyse national decision making on the critical issues confronting American Society. It was dedicated, in the words of its statement of purpose, to the task "of getting (these) diverse groups to work together . . . (and) to provide on specific problems concrete programmes for action planned in the best traditions of a functioning democracy." Such democratic planning, NPA believes, involves the development of effective governmental and private policies and programmes not only by official agencies but also through the independent initiative and cooperation of the main private-sector groups concerned. And, to preserve and strengthen American political and economic democracy, the necessary government actions have to be consistent with, and stimulate the support of, a dynamic private sector.

NPA brings together influential and knowledgeable leaders from business, labour, agriculture, and the applied and academic professions to serve on policy committees, of which the British-North American Committe is one. These committees identify emerging problems confronting the nation at home and abroad and seek to develop and agree upon policies and programmes for coping with them. The research and writing for these committees are provided by NPA's professional staff and, as required, by outside experts.

In addition, NPA's professional staff undertakes research designed to provide data and ideas for policy makers and planners in government and the private sector. These activities include the preparation on a regular basis of economic and demographic projections for the national economy, regions, states, and metropolitan areas; the development of programme planning and evaluation techniques; research on national goals and priorities; analysis of welfare and dependency problems, employment and manpower needs, education, medical care, environmental protection, energy, and other economic and social issues confronting American society; and studies of changing international realities and their implications for US policies.

NPA publications, including those of the British-North American Committee, can be obtained from the Association's office, 1606 New Hampshire Avenue, NW, Washington, DC 20009 (Tel: 202-265-7685).

The C.D. Howe Research Institute is a private, non-political, non-profit organization founded in January 1973, by the merger of the C.D. Howe Memorial Foundation and the Private Planning Association of Canada (PPAC), to undertake research into Canadian economic policy issues, especially in the areas of international policy and major government programmes.

HRI continues the activities of the PPAC. These include the work of three established committees, composed of agricultural, business, educational, labour, and professional leaders. The committees are the Canadian Economic Policy Committee, which has been concentrating on Canadian economic issues, especially in the area of trade, since 1961; the Canadian-American Committee, which has dealt with relations between Canada and the United States since 1957 and is jointly sponsored by HRI and the Nationl Planning Association in Washington; and the British-North American Committee, formed in 1969 and sponsored jointly by the National Planning Association, the British-North American Research Association in London and HRI. Each of the committees meets twice a year to consider important current issues and to sponsor and review studies that contribute to better public understanding of such issues.

In addition to taking over the publications of the three PPAC committees, HRI releases the work of its staff, and occasionally of outside authors, in four other publications: *Observations,* six or seven of which are published each year; *Policy Review and Outlook,* published annually; *Special Studies,* to provide detailed analysis of major policy issues for publication on an occasional basis; and *Commentaries,* to give wide circulation to the views of experts on issues of current Canadian interest.

HRI publications, including those of the British-North American Committee, are available from the Institute's offices, 2064 Sun Life Building, Montreal, Quebec H3B 2X7 (Tel: 514-879-1254).